Carpenters
Album-by-Album: So
A Retrospective by R

This book chronicles
Carpenters. Details will be given on the making of each album
and how each song was developed. Little known trivia and
important facts will be shared within these pages. Chart details
will be listed as well as Carpenters events and happenings at
the time each album was released.

Their music is now described as classic, and millions around
the world have enjoyed them for over 40 years. What is this
fascination the world continues to have with the Carpenters? Is
it the joy brought forth from Richard Carpenter's dazzling
musical arrangements? Or the chilling perfection and beauty of
Karen Carpenter's voice? There are many reasons for this
continued "love affair" the world has had with this duo. It's
easy to say that quality never goes out of style. The Carpenters
were the epitome of quality in music. Their popularity and
many accolades can attest to that.

In June 1963 the Carpenter family moved from New Haven,
Connecticut, to Downey, California. This move was going to
give Richard Carpenter the opportunity to expand his
knowledge and career in music. In 1964 he enrolled at
California State University, Long Beach. He started to refine his
piano techniques with his teacher, Frank Pooler. At the same
time Karen Carpenter began playing the drums in the Downey
High School marching band. By late 1965 they formed a jazz
trio called the Richard Carpenter Trio with their friend, Wes
Jacobs, who played the tuba. The trio met with early success
when they won the Hollywood Bowl Battle of the bands on
June 24, 1966. At the end of the show, Neely Plumb, the West
Coast manager of RCA Records, approached them with an offer
to record for RCA. They recorded several songs for RCA, which
were never released (although a few did show up in a
Carpenters boxed set retrospective).

In May of 1966, Richard Carpenter joined a midnight session in
Joe Osborn's garage studio to accompany a trumpeter who was
auditioning for Osborn's Magic Lamp record label. During this

session Karen was asked to sing, and Joe was immediately taken with her. He signed Karen as a solo artist. The label released a single featuring two Richard Carpenter compositions, "Looking for Love" and "I'll Be Yours." Due to limited funds and distribution, the single was not a hit, and Magic Lamp soon closed down. Osborn continued his musical union with Karen and Richard letting them record in his studio for several years afterward.

In 1967 Karen and Richard formed the band Spectrum with four of their friends from Long Beach State University. The group performed in many LA-based clubs, including the Whisky a Go-Go, but oftentimes met with negative response. LA club goers didn't know how to respond to Spectrum; the group disbanded in 1968.

By mid-1968 Karen and Richard returned to Joe Osborn's garage studio to cut a few tracks for a demo tape. Karen and Richard made their first television appearance on June 22, 1968, on "Your All American College Show." They performed a somewhat jazz inspired arrangement of Martha and the Vandellas' "Dancing in the Street" in which Karen sang lead vocals and played drums simultaneously. They ended up winning the competition. John Wayne (one of the judges on that particular episode) was so taken with Karen that he asked her to audition for a leading role in his upcoming movie, "True Grit."

In 1969 Richard and Karen signed a $50,000 a year contract with Ford Motor Company. They also each received a special Mustang.

After another round of sending their demo tape out, Carpenters again failed to get the attention of a record company. Their chances were looking dim. Finally, their demo landed in the hands of Herb Alpert (leader of the Tijuana Brass and co-founder of A&M Records) through a friend-of-a-friend of Karen and Richard's mom. Herb Alpert immediately fell in love with Karen's voice, saying, "It felt like her voice was on the couch, like she was sitting next to me. It was full and round, and it was *amazing*."

Highly impressed with Karen's voice, Richard's arrangements and their beautiful harmonies, Herb Alpert offered them a deal right at that moment. On April 22, 1969, Karen and Richard signed a contract with A&M Records.

Now Karen and Richard had to deal with the fact they had signed a $50,000 a year contract with the Ford Motor Company. Giving up a guaranteed $50,000 was going to be a hard thing to do, but A&M offered them the opportunity to create their own sound and share their unique talents with the world. With help from their friend, Thomas Balher, they were let out of their contract with Ford and were able to pursue their career with A&M Records.

This is where it all began...

Carpenters
Album by Album: Song by Song
A Retrospective by Rick Henry

Websites developed or owned by Rick Henry:
Online with Carpenters click here
LeadSister.com click here

Note from Rick Henry:
Before moving on I want to describe how this book is laid out. Within these pages there will be factual descriptions on the making of each album along with my own personal views/review on each interspersed. I will be giving each album a rating of 1 – 10 (of course, 10 being best). Myself being a fan it would be very easy for me to rate all Carpenters album a 9 or 10, but for the sake of giving an honest depiction of each album in the sense of popular music overall (not just the perspective of a Carpenters fan) I will rate each album as unbiased as I can. These ratings will come from a combination of sources and views including quality and strength of each individual song, how well the songs relate to each other, originality in musical and vocal arrangements, vocal performances, musical agility and precision, overall flow of the album, quality of recording, overall originality of the album, artwork and overall strength of the album in its entirety.

At the end of this book, I have included a list of my all-time favorite Carpenters tunes. Check it out. How does my list rate against your list?

One more last shout-out here: I want to give a very big thank you to Frank Rendo for helping to proofread this book. He spent countless hours going over details and adding quite a few interesting tidbits which I had overlooked. I also want to thank Irene Economou for doing a second proof- reading of the book to make sure it was 100% perfect. I also want to thank Irene for her help in making the Facebook group, Karen Carpenter Magazine, such a happening place on the Internet.

Offering (aka Ticket to Ride) (CLICK HERE to purchase)
Released: October 9, 1969
Producer: Jack Daugherty
Engineer: Ray Gerhardt
Vocals: Karen and Richard Carpenter
Drums: Karen Carpenter
Keyboards: Richard Carpenter
Guest Artist: Herb Alpert (shakers)
Bass: Joe Osborn, Bob Messenger, Karen Carpenter
Guitar: Gary Sims
Harp: Gayle Levant (Someday)
Art Director: Tom Wilkes
Photographer: Jim McCrary
Chart Positions: US #150 (1970), UK #20 (1972), #35 (1975), Japan #88, Australia 19
Singles: Ticket to Ride/Your Wonderful Parade: US #52, US AC #19
Rick Henry's Rating: 7.5

After being signed to A&M Records, Carpenters went to work on their debut album immediately and were given complete freedom in the studio to create their first album. Richard experimented with different musical genres and textures. He refined his skills with the vocal dubbing process, which he had been working on for the past few years. Once completed, "Offering" was to become a gem of innovation, which was largely overlooked by the music buying public. Carpenters were called "boring" by the Hollywood press and some staff at A&M; they really did not know how to market this brother and sister duo. After the failure of "Offering," it was expected (by several A&M executives and members of staff) that Carpenters would be dropped from the label fairly quick.

"Offering" was the prototype of what became Carpenters' signature sound. The album consisted of ideas, sounds and interests, which were later refined and explored on following albums. With "Offering," Richard Carpenter explored a range of curiosities from the standard ballad ("All of My Life") to choral vocals ("Invocation," "Benediction") to skeptical natured folk tunes ("Your Wonderful Parade," "Nowadays Clancy Can't Even Sing") to jumpy, jazz experiments ("All I Can Do") and more.

The album's standout track is Carpenters' retooling of the Beatles' "Ticket to Ride." The song helped to create a buzz in the entertainment industry. Industry insiders began to take note of the female drummer who sang like an angel.

The album was promoted on the Hollywood scene as Carpenters performed at the film premieres of "Goodbye, Mr. Chips" and "Hello, Dolly!" in December 1969. Leslie Bricusse, the composer of the musical score for "Goodbye, Mr. Chips," found Karen to be amazing. Karen was a hit with industry insiders and celebrities. Her image was memorable: a girl drummer gracefully singing. In an interview later, Briscusse mentioned that she was certainly the talking point of the night.

"Offering" did not chart in the US until after its rerelease in early 1971 when the album was repackaged and retitled to "Ticket to Ride." Finally, the album reached US #150 on March 13, 1971. The album also reached UK #20 in April 1972, and, in August 1975, re-entered the UK charts to reach #35 (this was during the time that "Horizon" was #1 on the UK charts).

The Songs:
1. Invocation (Richard Carpenter / John Bettis) 1:01
   This song is the first of two bookend pieces, which open and close the album. The word "invocation" is described as the act of calling on God. An a cappella offering, "Invocation" blends a multi-part, choir performance in

which all the vocals are done by Karen and Richard Carpenter. This is achieved by a process called overdubbing. Overdubbing is a system of recording sounds, instruments, or, in this case, voices and superimposing or stacking each on top of the other to create a layered effect. Overdubbing became a trademark sound of the Carpenters in the early 70's. Karen and Richard first recorded "Invocation" in 1968 in Joe Osborn's garage studio. Richard Carpenter has stated that this hymn was written as an expression of having fun overdubbing in an a cappella vein. The song's counterpart is "Benediction" which closes the album.

2. Your Wonderful Parade (Carpenter / Bettis) 2:54
This song opens with Richard's circus-style announcement and moves into a song powered by snare drum and harpsichord. It was released as the A-side of the (unsuccessful) first Carpenters single (yes, this was their first single release before "Ticket to Ride.") A few months later the single was rereleased with "Ticket to Ride" as the A-side.

John Bettis and Richard Carpenter wrote "Parade" in 1967 as somewhat of a rebellion against the "establishment," which they later became part of with their universal success. Karen and Richard first recorded the song in 1968 in Osborn's garage and rerecorded it in 1969 for the album "Offering."

This is one of several songs on this album to feature Richard Carpenter as the lead vocalist and incorporates a fantastic harmony vocal by Karen. Karen's and Richard's voices blend together beautifully. One of the highlights of the song is Karen's marching band drum solo at the end, which pans from one speaker through to the other, just as you would hear the parade as it marches by.

3. Someday (Carpenter / Bettis) 5:13
This hauntingly, beautiful ballad showcased a rough, yet dark and moody vocal by Karen Carpenter. This was a predecessor to what would become Karen's trademark

vocal style. She was only 19 when she recorded this song. Not many 19 year olds can sing with the same level of maturity and depth as Karen did. Karen was never satisfied with her vocal performance on this song and wanted to rerecord it. Overall, her performance is well done, although in a few parts of the song her voice is pitchy and strained, and she sings slightly off-key at times with a labored sound. She did, in fact, rerecord a portion of the song in 1980 as part of a medley for the television special "Music, Music, Music." The medley ended up in the boxed-set "From the Top," which was later renamed "The Essential Collection 1965-1997."

4. Get Together (Chet Powers) 2:36
   This song is headed by Richard's lead vocal and processed with an echo effect and backed by a multi-tracked chorus. The hallucinatory reverberations gave the song a somewhat psychedelic sound, which was popular in the late '60's. Some fans have commented the song would have been more effective with Karen performing the lead vocal.

   This classic was written by Chet Powers (aka Dino Valenti from the rock group, Quicksilver Messenger Service). An ode to peace and love, it was written right around the time the Civil Rights Act was signed into law in the US. The song was first recorded and released in June 1964 by the Kingston Trio for their album "Back in Town." By the time Carpenters recorded "Get Together" it had already been a hit twice, first by We Five in 1965 when they took it to #31 on the Billboard singles chart. And, in 1969, the Youngbloods took it into the top 5 after it was adopted as the theme for the National Council of Christians and Jews.

   Carpenters recorded a live version of this song in early 1970 with Karen handling the lead vocal for the "Your Navy Presents" radio show.

5. All of My Life (Richard Carpenter) 3:02
   This is an early indicator of what would become the Carpenters' trademark sound. It includes every aspect

of the Carpenters' classic sound: the overdubbed vocal choruses, Richard Carpenter's pristine musical arrangement, thoughtful lyrics and Karen's yearningly deep and dark vocals. Several fans have listed this song as a possible "missed opportunity" for release as a single.

Although Joe Osborn is credited as playing the bass guitar on this song, it was Karen who played the bass (she also plays drums). Joe Osborn taught Karen the fundamentals of the instrument of which she caught on quickly. Many Carpenters fans consider this to be the album's best track. In 1970 the song was used as the B-side to the classic hit "We've Only Just Begun."

"All of My Life" was written in 1967 and was included on the original demo tape, which Herb Alpert received in 1969.

Karen Carpenter nailed the vocals on this song. It's so incredibly dark: " *...Someone that I can call my own / Who'll come to my side when I am all alone...* " But it's also hopeful.

6. Turn Away (Carpenter / Bettis) 3:10
   This tune is a combination of two songs in one (as was 1975's "Only Yesterday"). The straightforward verses lead into a time signature change for the upbeat, multi-tracked vocal on the chorus. Richard sings this one with an exciting and youthful verve.

   "Turn Away" sports a fresh, pop sound, unlike many of the other tracks on the album, which are more influenced by the experimental jazz/crushed-harmony sound left over from the Carpenters' earlier band, Spectrum.

7. Ticket to Ride (John Lennon / Paul McCartney) 4:10
   From the very beginning, Karen and Richard have claimed to be fans of the Beatles. Before landing their contract with A&M, they recorded several Beatles songs

including "Nowhere Man" and "Can't Buy Me Love." It was only natural a Beatles tune was included on their debut album, and "Ticket to Ride" was reborn. Richard took the upbeat Beatles song and turned it into a melodious and reflective ballad.

Carpenters released "Ticket to Ride" as a single with "Your Wonderful Parade" as the B-side on November 5, 1969, and made its debut on Billboard's Hot 100 Singles Chart on February 14, 1970. By May 9th the song reached #54 and stayed on the chart for 12 weeks. It also reached #19 on Billboard's Adult Contemporary chart.

Karen's vocal presentation on this song was excellent, although there were points in which she seemed a bit uncomfortable, strained and even forced. She was still somewhat rough around the edges.
Richard's keyboard work and strings arrangement were outstanding and really set the brooding mood of the song. It was dark and light coming together to form a forest of emotions.

The music video for "Ticket to Ride" was filmed on March 2, 1970, (Karen's 20th birthday) in Squaw Valley, California, which is in the Lake Tahoe area. This is the same area in which they took the album cover pictures for the repackaged "Ticket to Ride" album cover... you know, that neat, boat picture.

While working on their first greatest hits album, "The Singles 1969-1973," Karen rerecorded both her lead vocal and drums. A guitar track was added, which was masterfully performed by Tony Peluso.

The Beatles' upbeat version of the song was a major hit around the world in 1965 having reached #1 in the US, UK, Canada, Australia, Ireland, Sweden and several other countries around the world. The songwriting credits list John Lennon and Paul McCartney as its authors, although John Lennon has claimed that he wrote the song himself with very little input from McCartney.

8. <u>Don't Be Afraid (Richard Carpenter)</u> 2:06
   This is one of many songs on the album that dates back to the pre-Carpenters days. It was originally written in 1968 and recorded in Joe Osborn's garage studio. The 1968 version was included on the demo, which was submitted to Herb Alpert. The lyrics "love is a groovy thing" and "sunshine and joy" along with the girl-group sound make this very much a period piece of the late 60's era, when peace and love were all the rage. The song received extra attention as the B-side to "For All We Know."

9. <u>What's the Use? (Carpenter / Bettis)</u> 2:43
   Richard sings lead vocal with Karen doing backup and harmony vocals in this song. The vocal arrangement is especially engaging as you listen to Karen humming in the background blending perfectly with each instrument, especially the horns. Richard Carpenter's keyboard work is particularly captivating as the sound of his piano spritely rolls through the opening of the song. About one and a half minutes into the song we're treated to a classic late 60's/early 70's trumpet solo. Overall, the song is simplistic in its message and arrangement, but quite effective in bringing upon a good-time feel. Once again this is very much a product of its time with its lazy afternoon feel.

10. <u>All I Can Do (Carpenters / Bettis)</u> 1:41
    This song is set to a complex 5/4 time signature, similar to what is heard on Dave Brubeck's 1961 hit, "Take Five." This quirky, avant-jazz tune contains delightful experimentations of musicality and unique rhythms. The song sports a creative, chunky, bass line performed by Joe Osborn, along with the lively and affective drum styling of Karen Carpenter. It eventually works into a fantastic keyboard solo by Richard – the song has a little bit of everything for everybody in just under two minutes. "All I Can Do" was initially recorded as an instrumental in 1967, during the Spectrum days. Later,

John Bettis wrote the lyrics for the song, becoming one of his earliest compositions with Carpenters.

- **Note from Rick Henry:** *This is my favorite song from "Offering." Many Carpenters fans write this song off as being boring, noisy or just plain offensive. I hear a good amount of creativity in this unusual little number. It appeals to my artistic and avant-garde side. I really dig those off-beat jazz tunes.*

11. Eve (Carpenter / Bettis) 2:52
    "...Wide as it may be /Reality is here among the stones..."
    Dramatic, dark, rich and soulfully mysterious, "Eve" is one of the album's highlights. Written in 1968, "Eve" was inspired by an episode of the British suspense thriller "Journey to the Unknown". The episode aired on September 26, 1968, starring Carol Lynley, and was titled "Eve." From this episode Richard shaped the dramatic musical and vocal arrangements. Karen's vocal performance is mournfully warm, deep and somber. At the young age of 19 Karen displays her ability to connect and communicate in such a way that reaches into your soul and tugs a bit. Karen displays her musical finesse by playing both the bass guitar and drums.

    - **Note from Rick Henry:** *"Eve" is a fan favorite as well as being one of my own personal favorites. I love it for its dark richness and the maturity of Karen's voice.*

12. Nowadays Clancy Can't Even Sing (Neil Young) 4:18
    This graceful, folk-rock ballad was written in the spring of 1965 by Neil Young and recorded for the 1966 debut album of his band, Buffalo Springfield. The song is filled with restless and unsettled ever-changing emotions. The basis of the song is steeped in feelings of rejection, something with which Karen Carpenter was able to identify. Some of the insights and emotions in this song were based on Neil's schoolboy friend who suffered with MS. The song was the debut single for Buffalo Springfield and reached #110 on the US charts. A year

later Buffalo Springfield hit it big reaching #7 in the US with the classic "For What It's Worth."

Choosing to record this song illustrates Richard Carpenter's range in musical tastes. He took Buffalo Springfield's "Nowadays Clancy Can't Even Sing" and radically reworked it. The song that was originally a display of 60's folk-psychedelic with hints of prog-rock was now a polished, progressively pop tune with lush layers of vocals. The interplay between Richard's reflective lead vocal and Karen's forlorn backup phrasing bring a texture to the song which jumps right out to the heart of the listener to captivate the darker, deeper side of the emotions of the heart. Most exciting is Richard's lively jazz-influenced keyboard solo, which fades out to the end of the song.

This being the last full-length song on the album made a bold statement in its breadth of emotion and musical competence. Right from the beginning the confidence Carpenters had was evident in their ability to create pop music which is detailed and focused on a series of complex emotions and textured musical layers.

- **Note from Rick Henry** – *Oftentimes I call this my favorite song from the album, though it does run a close second to "All I Can Do." I love the creativity and complexity of the song's arrangement. There are so many different textures in the song and is a treat to listen to with headphones on. I really enjoy the interchange of vocals between Karen and Richard. Karen's backing vocals really stand out and add a sense of the blues to the song.*

13. Benediction (Carpenter / Bettis) :43
    At 43 seconds this is the closing bookend companion to "Invocation" and includes the similar multi-layered, choir-like vocals. The word "benediction" is described as an invocation of divine blessing especially at the end of a religious service. Unlike "Invocation," "Benediction" includes an added strings arrangement plus a tolling bell, which gives the song an ethereal "church-like" feel.

Close to You (click here to purchase)
Released: August 19, 1970
Producer: Jack Daugherty
Arrangements & Orchestration: Richard Carpenter
All Vocals: Karen Carpenter & Richard Carpenter
Drums: Karen Carpenter and Hal Blaine
Keyboards: Richard Carpenter
Bass: Joe Osborn and Danny Woodhams
Woodwinds: Jim Horn, Bob Messenger, Doug Strawn
Harp: Gayle Levant
Engineer: Ray Gerhardt & Dick Bogert
Art Direction: Tom Wilkes
Photography: Kessel/Brehm Photography
Chart Positions: US #2/ UK #23/ Japan #53/ Australia #16/ Canada #1
Certifications: 2 x Multi-Platinum (RIAA)
Singles: (They Long to Be) Close to You/I Kept on Loving You, We've Only Just Begun/All of My Life (chart positions and release dates are listed in the song by song synopsis for this album)
Rick Henry's Rating: 9.4

Shortly after the lack of chart success with their first album, "Offering," Carpenters quickly began work on their second album. Going against the general consensus of A&M insiders, Herb Alpert gave them a second chance. Alpert recognized that with Carpenters he had an act with the potential to achieve an across-the-board commercial success. It was just a matter of recording the right song. The first two tracks to be recorded were "Love Is Surrender" and "I'll Never Fall in Love Again." Right from the beginning the direction of this second album was decidedly more contemporary then "Offering."

Once the song "(They Long to Be) Close to You" became a hit, A&M put the pressure on Carpenters to complete this album in order to capitalize on their current success. They finished the album quickly including new recordings of four songs from their earlier Spectrum days. The result was an album, which would catapult Carpenters into superstardom.

The album was immensely popular having reached #2 on the Billboard Top 200 (staying on the chart for 87 weeks) and sold over two million copies along with winning the 1970 Best New Artist Grammy Award. In 2003 the album was ranked #175 on Rolling Stone Magazine's 500 Greatest Albums of All Time.

- **Note from Rick Henry:** *I give this album a rating of 9.4 predominantly for its creativity and versatility. This album showcases the diverse talents of this young group very well. It's a catalyst of a direction they should have dug into a little further.*

1. <u>We've Only Just Begun (Paul Williams / Roger Nichols)</u> 3:04 *"White lace and promises /A kiss for luck and we're on our way"...* Released as a single on August 21, 1970, "We've Only Just Begun" became an instant classic with its optimistic outlook. It reached #2 (for four weeks) in the US , #28 in the UK, #71 in Japan, #1 in Canada, #6 in Australia. In the US the song was certified Gold for selling over one million copies (which nowadays would be equivalent to platinum status).

   The song began its life in a television commercial for Crocker Bank. The commercial showed a young couple getting married, and then driving off into the sunset, while "We've Only Just Begun" played over it. Paul Williams sang the song in the commercial. Originally, Tony Asher (who co-wrote many of the songs featured on the Beach Boys' classic "Pet Sounds" album) was commissioned to write music for the ad agency that did the Crocker Bank commercial. At the time they were working on this commercial, Asher suffered a broken arm from a skiing accident and was unavailable. Upon Asher's suggestion Paul Williams and Roger Nichols were hired for the job. The agency made it clear to Williams that they did not want a jingle. They wanted their commercial to be a mini-movie (what we now know as a music video). Williams and Nichols wrote the first two verses of the song and a bridge. They also wrote a third verse (which was not used in the commercial) just in case somebody would want to record the song. One late (and sleepless) night Richard Carpenter had the television on, and the song caught his attention as it played throughout the commercial. The next day he phoned Paul Williams and asked if there was a complete song. Paul Williams says fortunately they did have a complete song, but even if there wasn't one he would have lied and then sat down and written it.

The song has gone on to become one of modern music's most popular wedding songs and was also used as the class song by many graduating classes of 1971. The sheet music itself has sold well over three million copies.

"We've Only Just Begun" was Carpenters' third official single release and their second smash hit, the follow-up to "(They Long to Be) Close to You." As the years have passed the song has been dubbed their signature song.

- **Note from Rick Henry:** *Had Tony Asher not broken his arm "We've Only Just Begun" would never have been written.*

2. Love Is Surrender (Ralph Carmichael) 1:59
   The chorus in Ralph Carmichael's original contemporary Christian composition of the song was *"Love is surrender; you must surrender to His Will."* Richard Carpenter changed it to *"you must surrender if you care"* to fit the pop music theme of the album.

   Ralph Carmichael is a popular contemporary Christian composer and arranger. His first big break was in the late 1950's when he provided the arrangements for Nat King Cole's "The Magic of Christmas" which was released in 1960. He continued his work with Cole until his untimely death in 1965. After Cole's passing Ralph Carmichael wrote arrangements for Ella Fitzgerald, Stan Kenton, Bing Crosby, Jack Jones, Peggy Lee and a host of others. He was also the Musical Director for the sitcom

"I Love Lucy" during the show's later years. In 1958 Carmichael wrote the score for the science fiction film "The Blob."

His foray into Christian music started in the 1960's. His work which consisted of a pop-rock sound, earned him recognition as the Father of Contemporary Christian Music. Elvis Presley recorded Carmichael's hymn "Reach Out to Jesus" in 1971.

The shared lead vocal by Karen and Richard again reinforces the natural blending of their voices, which works very well with the multi-tracked background vocals (which of course are all done by Karen and Richard). Richard discovered the song in the mid-1960's while attending California State University in Long Beach. Longtime Carpenters associate, Doug Strawn, asked Richard to play keyboards for a choir. The regular accompanist was unavailable that evening. One of the songs the choir performed was Ralph Carmichael's "Love Is Surrender." Richard was quickly impressed with the song, and he kept it in his repertoire of songs he and Karen would perform. When it came time to record it for A&M records the lyrics were changed to accommodate the nature of the music Carpenters were recording.

- **Note from Rick Henry:** *One of my favorite aspects of this song is the sprightly electric keyboard riff, which Richard Carpenter plays throughout. You can also hear a similar piano riff throughout the "Bacharach/David Medley" which was recorded in 1971 for their album "Carpenters."*

3. Maybe It's You (Richard Carpenter/John Bettis) 3:04
   This song dates back to 1968 during Karen and Richard's Spectrum days. *"Maybe it's you, maybe it's me. Maybe it's just the constant rhythm of the sea."* With its dreamy lyric and swirling orchestration the song conjures images of walks along the "waves of velveteen."

Karen displays a warmth and maturity in her vocals far beyond her young age of 20. She sang this song with perfect clarity while maintaining a sense of familiarity in her comforting voice.

Many music critics considered this song strong enough to have been released as a single. Though the song was never released as an A-side, it was released as the B-side to the single "Hurting Each Other" on December 23, 1971.

- **Note from Rick Henry** – *this is amongst my 15 most favorite Carpenters tunes.*

4. Reason to Believe (Tim Hardin) 3:03
   Prior to the Carpenters this Tim Hardin classic had been covered by several artists including The Youngbloods, Rick Nelson, Peter Paul & Mary, Glen Campbell and others. Rod Stewart's version was released about six months after Carpenters release. Tim Hardin also wrote the classic tune "If I Were a Carpenter," which was a hit for both Bobby Darin and Johnny Cash.

   After "We've Only Just Begun" peaked on the charts, Karen and Richard considered releasing "Reason to Believe" as a single. The song was getting a good amount of radio airplay and was favorably received by fans. Instead, they opted to release "For All We Know," which was from their upcoming album, "Carpenters." About the song's arrangement, Richard Carpenter has said if he had thought of it at the time he would have added a steel guitar somewhere in the song. Carpenters recording featured a country flair to it with a somewhat mournful reading by Karen Carpenter.

5. Help! (John Lennon/Paul McCartney) 3:03
   This song was originally scheduled to be released as the Carpenters' follow-up single to "Ticket to Ride," which enjoyed minor chart success in the spring of 1970. But before it was released, "Close to You" was recorded and chosen for the second single instead.

Until "Close to You" came around, the song "Help!" had been slated for release as the second single. Some people speculate this would have made Carpenters appear to be a Beatles cover band. My own personal guess is that "Help!" would have most likely reached the Top 40. It would have not been a huge hit, but would have been enough to garner decent airplay and sales.

As with "Ticket to Ride," Richard Carpenter molded "Help!" into their own song. Instead of guitars, Richard Carpenter used the harpsichord to drive this song. Karen Carpenter sings this one with confidence and upbeat exuberance. She was able to mix hints of opposing emotions into her delivery with feelings of angst and mournful longing. Carpenters really get the groove and rock out on this excellent rendition of "Help!"

"Help!" was the Beatles' follow-up single to "Ticket to Ride." Both songs reached #1 in 1965 in the US, UK, Australia, Canada, Sweden, Ireland and several other countries around the world. "Help!" has been covered by many artists including Deep Purple, Dolly Parton and Tina Turner.

6. (They Long to Be) Close to You (Burt Bacharach/Hal David) 4:33   Burt Bacharach was so impressed when he heard Carpenters' recording of "Ticket to Ride" that he invited them to perform at a benefit concert for the Reiss-Davis Clinic. The concert was happening on February 26, 1970, and Bacharach asked Karen and Richard to perform a medley of his tunes. Immediately Richard got to work in arranging an early version of the Bacharach/David Medley. During this process Herb Alpert brought the song "They Long to Be Close to You" and asked Richard to include it in the medley. Ultimately, Richard decided the song did not fit in with the flow of the medley. With continued encouragement from Herb, Richard decided to record the song as a stand-alone track. The group worked hard on getting the right sound for the song. They recorded several

takes before everyone was satisfied. This was the first Carpenters recording to feature Hal Blaine on drums. It was said he was brought in to put more muscle into the sound of the drums and to give Karen the opportunity to focus on her vocals more.

When asked how he thought the song would do, Richard commented it would either hit #1 or fail all together – no in-between. The song was shortened by 53 seconds (from the album version) for the single release. The album version fades out and then comes back with continued "waaaah" vocals. Richard changed the song title to "(They Long to Be) Close to You."

"Close to You" was Carpenters' second single and was released on May 15, 1970. It reached #1 on July 25, 1970, and stayed on top for four weeks (on the US Billboard chart). The single sold nearly two million copies and was certified Gold (in 1970, platinum records were not awarded, if so it would have been certified Platinum).

The single "(They Long to Be) Close to You" was initially released as a double A-side with "I Kept on Loving You" as the B-side. A&M left it up to radio programmers to choose their preferred song. As history has it, the choice was made quickly, and "Close to You" became an overnight smash hit.

Bacharach had given the song to Alpert to record as a follow-up to his 1968 #1 hit "This Guy's in Love With You," but Alpert felt the song was not right for him. One of the earliest recordings of the song was featured on Dionne Warwick's 1964 album "Make Way for Dionne Warwick." Richard Chamberlain included "They Long to Be Close to You" on his 1963 album "Twilight of Honor" and was used as the B-side of his single "Blue Guitar."

Burt Bacharach and Hal David have composed many great tunes including "Wives and Lovers," "Alfie," "Walk On By," "Trains and Boats and Planes," "What the World Needs Now Is Love," "I'll Never Fall in Love Again," "The

Look of Love," "This Guy's in Love with You," "A House Is Not a Home," "Do You Know the Way to San Jose," "Raindrops Keep Falling on My Head," "I Say a Little Prayer," "Always Something There to Remind Me," "One Less Bell to Answer," "What's New, Pussycat?" "The Man Who Shot Liberty Valance," and several others.

- **Note from Rick Henry:** *In researching this song I came to discover that in the process of creating "(They Long to Be) Close to You," Carpenters recorded it several times. I would very much love to hear some of those early outtakes. There are three recordings in existence; the first was Karen singing in a Harry Nilsson style in which she forcibly accents the word "you." The second was done with Hal Blaine on drums and Larry Knechtel on piano, but was scrapped as his performance was too harsh for the feel of the song. However, for the third arrangement (which is the one that made it on the album), Hal Blaine was kept on drums.*

7. <u>Baby It's You (Mack David / Burt Bacharach / Barney Williams)</u> 2:50 The Shirelles reached the US top ten with the song in 1961 and then in 1969, the Los Angeles based rock group named Smith took the song into the top five, scoring an even bigger hit with it. Figuring more prominently into the picture of Carpenters' music, "Baby It's You" was also recorded by the Beatles and released on their 1963 chart topping debut album "Please, Please Me."

Originally "Baby It's You" was written as "I'll Cherish You" but was rewritten by the request of Luther Dixon (aka Barney Williams) who produced the track for the Shirelles. Barney Williams is a pen name used by Luther Dixon. Dixon was an American songwriter, producer and singer. He helped develop the key sound of the girl group, The Shirelles. He also co-wrote hits such as The Crests' "16 Candles," The Platters' "With This Ring" and several others.

Also in the songwriting credits for "Baby It's You" is Mack David. Mack David is Hal David's older brother. Hal David wrote the lyrics for the majority of Burt Bacharach's compositions throughout the 60's and early 70's. Mack David (as with his brother Hal) had been on the music scene long before he ever teamed with Bacharach. Mack David is best known for his musical contributions to the Disney films "Cinderella" and "Alice in Wonderland." In the late 1940's he wrote an English version of Edith Piaf's "La Vie En Rose" which has appeared on many subsequent Edith Piaf compilations.

This soulful, dark song fits Karen's gutsy and full-bodied vocal perfectly.

8. I'll Never Fall in Love Again (Burt Bacharach / Hal David) 2:57

By the time Carpenters recorded this Bacharach/David classic (first introduced in 1968 in the musical "Promises, Promises") it had already been a hit twice. Bobby Gentry took the song to #1 in the UK in October 1969 and Dionne Warwick reached #6 on the US charts in January 1970.

One of the songs most enduring highlights is the opening line in which Karen and Richard's voices have been stacked over and over building up to a 39 voice chorus. They chant the opening line "here to remind you" four times with a groovy bass line behind their voices. From there, Karen takes over the song adding the sweet-filled determination of character in her voice. About one minute and fifty seconds into the song they repeat that opening chorus again with the buildup of 39 voices. With its echoing effects and layered voices, the vocal arrangement was cutting edge for its day; this was a new and fresh sound in 1970.

One fan has mentioned her favorite part of the song is the back and forth harmonies between Karen and Richard when they sing "out of those chain, those chains that bind you." (This can be found at about one minute and forty five seconds into the song).

9. <u>Crescent Noon (Richard Carpenter / John Bettis)</u> 4:10

"Crescent Noon" is one of four songs on the album that was written back in the Spectrum days. After the success of the single "Close to You," A&M Records was anxious to get an album on the market by Carpenters. Karen and Richard rushed the album out within a matter of weeks. In order to save time, they recorded their Spectrum songs which include "Maybe It's You," "Mr. Guder," "Another Song" and the dark and haunting "Crescent Noon."

This song is a huge favorite of Carpenters fans - it could be Karen's deep and melancholy reading of the song that digs into the soul of the listener. One fan describes the song as having a "dreamy-like quality." This is perhaps one of the Carpenters' most expressive lyrics. It speaks of contrasting seasons, the breaking of the morning sun, and hopeful discovery. Karen's vocal performance excels as she uses her full range from deep, down, low and dark to her uppermost angelic tones. In the chorus Karen's voice is superbly blended with Richard's to produce an almost eerie, yet delightful sound.

- **Note from Rick Henry:** *"Crescent Noon" is one of those songs I skipped over for years and years. I'd listen to it occasionally but it never was a favorite. Then it must have been around 2005 that I began really giving the song a good, close listen, mostly due to conversations on <u>Carpenters Avenue Forum</u>. It was other fans that got me listening to the song. It now sits within my most favorite tunes by Carpenters. I just cannot resist her hauntingly, deep, dark vocals in this song.*

10. <u>Mr. Guder (Richard Carpenter / John Bettis)</u> 3:15

"Mr. Guder" is one of the most captivatingly creative songs ever recorded by Carpenters. It's a jazz-influenced tune with a strong, early 70's pop sensibility.

Richard and John worked at Disneyland's Coke Corner

during the summer of 1967. Their boss was Vic Guder; he was strict in enforcing Disneyland's policies as to proper etiquette and music selection to be played at Coke Corner. Richard and John scoffed at the policies and would sneak in some rock-pop tunes in between the tunes they were required to play. The last straw was Richard and John combing their hair in the park, upon which they got fired. In response, they wrote this tune. Richard is now apologetic about the song saying Guder was only doing his job.

This was used as the B-side of the November 20, 1970, release of the single "Merry Christmas, Darling."

One of the most remarkable parts of the song is the vocal arrangement. Karen sings the song with a cool sort of edge to her voice. The vocal trade-off near the end of the song is outstanding, showcasing a jazz type vocal that one may hear on a Manhattan Transfer album.

- **Note from Rick Henry:** *For some reason the feel of this song always makes me think of ocean waves and smooth sailing.*

11.   I Kept on Loving You (Roger Nichols / Paul Williams)
2:14

Richard took over on lead vocals for this song with some nice harmonizing done by Karen. This bright and energetic song is generally considered to be the best of the songs featuring Richard on lead vocal. Some fans have even hinted that this might have made a decent single. This was the first of five Paul Williams/Roger Nichols songs recorded by Carpenters.

"I Kept on Loving You" was recorded during the first sessions for the "Close to You" album, and it became the B-side to the mega-hit "(They Long to Be) Close to You." Paul Williams has stated that "I Kept on Loving You" got that free ride that every songwriter dreams of being the B-side of a huge hit. Paul Williams and Roger Nichols collected a nice sum of royalties for that one, but not even close to what they collected from "We've Only Just Begun."

"I Kept on Loving You" was also recorded by a group named Skin in 1970. It was the B-side to the single "Out in the Country," another song written by Williams and Nichols, which ended up being a hit for Three Dog Night.

12.   <u>Another Song (Richard Carpenter / John Bettis</u> (4:23)
This is one of those few tunes that Carpenters fans are split on. Some consider this to be one of Carpenters' best works; others ignore it all together and don't care for it.

As described on Wikipedia the song is constructed in three movements: a pop section (0:00-1:45), a medieval-influenced section (1:45-2:28) and a jazz section (2:28-4:23). The song opens with a short prelude based on "And, lo! The angel of the Lord came upon them" from Part One of Handel's "Messiah."

The song, which dates back to their Spectrum days, starts out with Karen's crystal clear vocal delivery as she sings the perils of a lost love. Karen's vocal begins tender and delicate but works into a cry of a yearning intensity. Slowly the music works gracefully into a well thought out thunderstorm of music where each instrument carefully portrays the emotions of emptiness and forlorn love. The song ends sounding like a master jam performed in a similar vein as what you may hear from The Mahavishnu Orchestra.

Karen not only performs lead vocals on this song but also masterfully shows her jazz-influenced chops on the drums.

"Another Song" is one of several recorded by Carpenters which displays their unique and versatile talents. The breadth of their musical spectrum crosses over a wider scope than most realize.

- **Note from Rick Henry:** *This is one of those very few songs that I can put the headphones on and listen to three or four times over. It's such a fascinating and thrilling musical piece.*

<u>Carpenters (click here to purchase)</u>
Released: May 14, 1971
Producer: Jack Daugherty
Arrangements & Orchestration: Richard Carpenter
All Vocals: Karen Carpenter & Richard Carpenter
Drums: Karen Carpenter and Hal Blaine
Keyboards: Richard Carpenter, Doug Strawn
Bass: Joe Osborn, Bob Messenger
Woodwinds and Reeds: Jim Horn, Bob Messenger, Doug Strawn
Harp: Gayle Levant
Harmonica: Tommy Morgan
Engineer: Ray Gerhardt & Dick Bogert
Assistant Engineer: Norm Kinney
Art Direction: Roland Young
Photography: Guy Webster
Chart Positions: US #2/ UK #11/ Japan #47/ Australia #16/ Canada #6
Certifications: 4 x Multi-Platinum (RIAA)
Singles: For All We Know/Don't Be Afraid, Rainy Days and Mondays/Saturday, Superstar/Bless the Beasts and Children (chart positions and release dates are listed in the song by song synopsis for this album)
Rick Henry's Rating: 8.9

Hot on the heels of the success of the "Close to You" album, "Carpenters" is released. In its time "Carpenters" was only one of two albums to contain three or more Top Three US Hits on it. The other was Blood, Sweat & Tears' 1969 album titled "Blood, Sweat and Tears." This record was soon broken by 1978 with mega-hits albums like "Grease" and "Saturday Night Fever" and then again in the 80's with albums by Michael Jackson and Madonna.

"Carpenters" achieved a couple of key milestones for Carpenters. First, it strengthened Karen's credibility as one of her generation's finest pop vocalists. Second, the album won a Grammy Award for Best Pop Vocal Performance by a Duo or Group (this was Carpenters' third and last Grammy Award). To date "Carpenters" remains their best-selling studio album in the US.

Many fans refer to the album as "The Tan Album," because the original album cover, with its overlapping flap, looked like an oversized, tan envelope. This has presumably been regarded as a play on The Beatles' album, "The Beatles," which has been nicknamed "The White Album."

Rock music critics gave this album lukewarm reviews, although in response to this album, Rolling Stone Magazine commented that, "the Carpenters have more going for them than against."

- **Note from Rick Henry:** *I gave this album a rating of 8.9 (a slight step down from "Close to You") for two main reasons. Although the music is produced to the finest detail and Karen's vocals are crystal clear pitch perfect, the album lacks a sense of originality. Whereas "Close to You" took chances in creativity with songs such as "Crescent Noon" and "Another Song," the album "Carpenters" plays it safe with songs which are more suited to receiving commercial AM radio play. Also, the album includes the filler cuts "Saturday" and "Druscilla Penny," which if replaced by songs featuring Karen's lead vocals would have made the album near perfect. The Bacharach/David Medley is a true treat and a fan favorite, although the album would have been greatly improved had Karen and Richard chosen the two best songs from the medley and recorded full-length versions (maybe "Knowing When to Leave" and "Make It Easy on Yourself").*

1.   Rainy Days and Mondays (Paul Williams / Roger Nichols) 3:36

"Carpenters" opens on a very strong note with the classic "Rainy Days and Mondays." After the mega-hit "We've Only Just Begun," Paul Williams catapulted to the top of Richard Carpenters list of songwriters to cover. The "Tan Album" includes two Williams/Nichols songs, "Rainy Days and Mondays" and "Let Me Be the One." Both songs had equal potential for hit single status, but it was "Rainy Days and Mondays" that was chosen to be the group's fifth single. "Rainy Days and Mondays" became an anthem of sorts in the 70's. People chanted the lines of the song, and radio stations played it for years to come whenever there was a rainy day on a Monday.

"Rainy Days and Mondays" was originally presented to The 5th Dimension, but they passed on recording the song. It was Richard Carpenter who found a goldmine in the song while sorting through a stack of demos submitted to him.

Released on April 23, 1971, "Rainy Days and Mondays" was the second single release from the "Tan Album" (it was also the second Williams / Nichols composition Carpenters took into the Top Two in less than a year). Although the song was a huge hit in both the US and Canada (reaching #2 and #3 respectively) the song hardly made a dent in other parts of the world, reaching #35 in Australia and #72 in Japan. The song did not chart in the UK until 1993 as a reissue when it made it to #63. The song sold over a million copies in the US and was certified Gold by the RIAA. The B-side to the single was "Saturday."

All the classic Carpenters trademarks are present including Tony Morgan's harmonica and Bob Messenger's soulful sax work. Many Carpenters fans consider this to be one of Karen's finest and strongest vocal works.

A few of the words fans have used to describe "Rainy Days and Mondays" include: supreme, sad, classic, emotional, deep, outstanding, soulful, dark, majestic, favorite, mood, introspective, magic, mournful, perfection, stunning, expressive, heartbreaking, amazing, passion…

- **Note from Rick Henry:** *Back in the 70's, I must have played this song thousands of times, and, to this day, I still listen to it on a fairly regular basis. This is one of those songs that will never die out. It is one of those all-time classics.*

2. <u>Saturday (Richard Carpenter / John Bettis)</u> 1:18
This is a Richard Carpenter lead vocal with Karen providing harmony vocals. This song is an ode to the joys of completing a long work/school week and looking forward to the ensuing weekend. The song certainly has its attributes: it's an upbeat and joyful feel-good tune; we can always use more of those. On the down side, this short tune (almost seems like a television jingle) follows "Rainy Days and Mondays," one of Carpenters' most powerful songs. Although pairing these songs one right after the other is an interesting contrast, it does, however, seem to stifle the momentum of the album going from a super powerful song right into a short, fluffy, filler song. The album would have maintained a stronger sense of continuity had they followed "Rainy Days" with "Let Me Be the One."

"Saturday" goes back to the Spectrum days and was written in 1967. It was used as the theme for many weekend radio and television programs. The song was also chosen to be the B-side of "Rainy Days and Mondays."

- **Note from Rick Henry:** *On further inspection of teaming "Rainy Days and Mondays" and "Saturday" back-to-back on the album and as a single, I came to realize that this teaming of the songs shows a contrast between the sad and mournful Monday vs. the happy and uplifting weekend. I especially enjoy the harmony vocals between Karen and Richard that adds a nice touch.*

3. <u>Let Me Be the One (Paul Williams / Roger Nichols)</u> 2:24

-

For over 30 years fans have been saying this song should have been a single and categorize it as a "missed opportunity." Richard had considered releasing it, but "Superstar" won out instead. He's stated he feels the song would have been a hit had it been released as a single. "Let Me Be the One" reinforces the fact that many of Carpenters' album tracks were equally as strong as their hit singles.

This Paul Williams classic made it to Richard Carpenter in the same stack of demos with "Rainy and Mondays." Richard Carpenter has expressed his appreciation of Karen's intimate reading, especially in the bridge.

- **Note from Rick Henry:** *I especially love the horns in this song. I've always felt this one would have made a good James Bond theme.*

4. <u>(A Place to) Hideaway (Randy Sparks)</u> 3:39
This song has an interesting background. Randy Sparks, the founder of the popular big folk chorus group The New Christie Minstrels, wrote it. Soon after the success of The New Christie Minstrels, Sparks opened the club, Ledbetters, as a source to discover and hone musicians for his group. Sparks wrote this song in 1968. After he finished writing it, he performed it for Michael Johnson, who was recording in one of Sparks' offices that day. You may remember Michael Johnson for his mid-to-late 70's hits "Bluer Than Blue" and "This Night Won't Last Forever." After hearing the song, Johnson commented that it was a bit trite, especially the lyrics "save my pennies for a rainy day." Regardless of Johnson's viewpoint on the song, Sparks decided to try it out in front of an audience at Ledbetters. He performed it, and the audience applauded him. Though, Sparks has mentioned that the audience would have applauded anything and anyone; that's just the type of audience they were. Sparks decided that Michael Johnson was right about the song, and he never performed it again.

Here is a quote taken from the e-book "The Carpenters Online Interviews" as spoken by Randy Sparks:

"About 1971...maybe 1972... can't remember for sure, after I had sold Ledbetter's and moved my family to our ranch in Northern California, I received a call from A&M Records one day. The question was, 'Do you own a song called Hideaway?' My answer was, 'no.' 'Well,' the person on the telephone said, 'Richard Carpenter thinks it's your song, and he learned it from you. He thinks he has most of it right, but isn't sure of a couple of words.' 'That's ridiculous!' I said. 'You obviously have some wires crossed somewhere. Did he say where it was that he learned it from me?' 'Ledbetter's,' was the reply. Then, all at once, I saw the whole picture a bit more clearly, but this kind of thing never happens in real life, does it? I had given Karen and Richard's group, The Spectrum, their first job (at least that's what I was told at the time), and they were the headliners during that week when I performed 'A Place to Hideaway' in public that one and only time. Richard hadn't said anything to me about the song, but he obviously liked it, and he has an incredible ear...and memory. He knew the whole song!"

Many fans cherish this song calling it a favorite from the album. Fans of this song say they can relate to the song's sense of longing and pain. The lyrics and Karen's voice speak to the soul.

This song contains one of the Carpenters' most commonly, misheard lyrics. Many fans and almost every lyrics website claim the lyric to be:

>*Bright colored pinwheels go round in my head*
>*I run through the mist of the wine*

When in actuality the lyric is:

>*Bright colored pinwheels go round in my head*
>*I run through the mist of the wind*

The confusion in the lyric stems from Karen's mispronunciation of the word "wind" pronouncing it "wind", such as "wind the watch," instead of pronouncing it as "wind," a gust of wind.

5.   For All We Know (Fred Karlin / Robb Wilson /Arthur James) 2:35

In late 1970, while on tour in Canada (opening for Engelbert Humperdinck), upon the suggestion of their manager, Sherwin Bash, Karen and Richard took a break to watch the movie "Lovers and Other Strangers." This modest comedy which features stars such as Bea Arthur, Cloris Leachman and Diane Keaton follows the life of a young couple living together. In one scene, during the couple's wedding, the song "For All We Know" is played as performed by Larry Meredith. The song caught Richard's attention, and Carpenters quickly recorded and released the song. The result was another chart-topping hit. Along with being a huge hit, the song also won an Academy Award for Best Song of 1970 (this was largely due to Carpenters' recording of the song).

But wait, there's a little more to the story of "For All We Know." It has to do with the trio that wrote the song. "For All We Know" was written by Fred Karlin, Robb Wilson and Arthur James. Fred Karlin's career began in the 1950's when he composed musical arrangements for Benny Goodman and Harry James. He scored an album featuring Kaye Ballard in the part of Lucy reading excerpts from the comic strip "Peanuts." He also co-wrote "Come Saturday Morning," which was a Top 20 hit for the Sandpipers in 1970. "For All We Know" is Karlin's biggest success. Robb Wilson and Arthur James have a slightly more interesting story. Robb Wilson and Arthur James met in 1967 from a mutual friend. But, before I go on with this story, there's a small twist here. Robb Wilson's name is actually Robb Royer and Arthur James' name is really James Arthur Griffin. After meeting in 1967, Royer and Griffin began collaborating together writing songs. In 1968 they formed the pop group Bread with lead singer David Gates. It was in 1970, after Bread had a huge hit with "Make It with You," that Griffin and Royer teamed with Fred Karlin under the pseudonyms of Wilson and James to write "For All We Know." The song was never recorded by Bread, but a recording of it by James Griffin shows up on the Bread compilation "Retrospective."

"For All We Know" charted quite well throughout the world reaching #3 in the US, #5 in Canada, #10 Australia and #18 UK. The song was also certified Gold by the RIAA for selling more than 1 million copies.

6. Superstar (Leon Russell / Bonnie Bramlett) 3:49
    "Superstar" is a classic amongst classics, even in the Carpenters catalog. This is the first of several Leon Russell songs Carpenters have recorded. Co-writer Bonnie Bramlett was part of the husband and wife team Delaney & Bonnie and Friends, their biggest hit is 1971's "Never Ending Song of Love."

    "Superstar" was first recorded in 1969 by Delaney and Bonnie and was used as the B-side of their single "Comin' Home" (at the time the song was called "Groupie (Superstar)." In 1970 Rita Coolidge recorded the song for Joe Cocker's A&M album "Mad Dogs and Englishmen."

    Richard, though, first heard the song performed by Bette Midler on the "Tonight Show." Though Midler's rendition of the song was much different from Carpenters' general style, Richard heard the potential in the song and decided to record it.

    The lyric in the song (about a groupie) was originally written, *"And I can hardly wait to sleep with you again."* Richard felt that line was a bit too risqué for a Carpenters record and changed the line to, *"And I can hardly wait to be with you again."*

    "Superstar" is considered to be one of Karen's finest vocal performances. Karen's vocal was recorded in one take as she read the lyrics from a napkin. Richard felt the vocal of this work lead was so good that he put it on the album. There was no reason to do a second take. A work lead is a vocal used as a guide for the other musicians and then is usually re-recorded once all the music is completed.

"Superstar" is a highly celebrated song having made it on too many "best of" charts throughout the decades, as well as being recorded by Luther Vandross and Sonic Youth, the latter recording included on the Carpenters tribute album "If I Were a Carpenter." The song also garnered Richard Carpenter a Grammy award nomination for Best Arrangement Accompanying Vocalist for this song. It was the second of five nominations Richard received for his arrangements. He didn't win any, although this is an impressive accomplishment. The song has also appeared in the Chris Farley & David Spader movie "Tommy Boy" as well as Nicholas Cage's "Ghost Rider."

Like Carpenters' previous four singles, "Superstar" was certified Gold status by the RIAA for selling more than a million copies. "Superstar" was Carpenters' first Top Ten hit in Japan having reached #7. Elsewhere in the world the song charted extremely well, #2 US, #3 Canada, #7 Japan, #18 UK, #21 Netherlands, #35 Australia.

"Bless the Beasts and Children" was the B-side of "Superstar." The song was hugely successful as a B-side, but you can read more about it in the review for the album "A Song for You."

Singer/Songwriter Leon Russell has also written the tunes "Delta Lady (Rita Coolidge), "Hummingbird" (B.B. King), "Bluebird" (Helen Reddy), "Back to the Island" (Captain & Tennille) and several others.

7. <u>Druscilla Penny (Richard Carpenter / John Bettis)</u> 2:14
    Although this is an interestingly, tasty little tune, this album would have been more consistent had it been replaced with another Karen Carpenter lead, maybe a nice studio recording of "And When He Smiles." "Druscilla Penny" would have been more effective being released as a non-LP B-side. That being said, I do enjoy the song.

The lyric of the hopeless groupie is both a put-down and a reaching-out. Richard Carpenter's flourishing harpsichord adds a darkness and mystique to the song. Richard's delivery as a lead vocalist is adequate, while Karen's harmonizing vocals really adds a shine to the song. The song manages to carry an alluring, dry and dark sense of humor about it.

8. <u>One Love (Richard Carpenter / John Bettis)</u> 3:23
Richard (and John Bettis) wrote "One Love" in 1967 when they worked at Disneyland's Coke Corner (Anaheim, CA). The song was originally titled "Candy" named after a waitress who worked at one of Disneyland's restaurants. Later it was changed to "One Love" and was given that Carpenters stamp of quality musicianship.

Karen's sincere and emotion-filled vocal performance is the main factor in driving this song which falls somewhere between very good and average on the scale of Carpenters tunes.

The lyrics *"Few are the choices we are given/ The sands of time pass quickly by"* is referenced on the inner sleeve of the "Voice of the Heart" collection.

"One Love" was used as the B-side to the 1974 single release of "I Won't Last a Day Without You."

9. <u>Bacharach/David Medley</u> 5:25
Early on in their career, Carpenters became the masters of the medley, when they would perform medleys of hits by other groups and songwriters. Once they amassed their own hits they began performing medleys of their songs. The Bacharach/David Medley is their first to be released and contains the following Burt Bacharach & Hal David songs: "Knowing When to Leave," "Make It Easy on Yourself," "(There's) Always Something There to Remind Me," "I'll Never Fall in Love Again," "Walk on By" and "Do You Know the Way to San Jose." In just under five and a half minutes Karen and

Richard successfully captured the essence of each of these six classic tunes.

A longer version of this medley exists which contains longer versions of each song as well as a few extras including "Baby It's You" and "Any Day Now." This longer medley is more relaxed and quite a refreshing listen. The extended medley can be found on the Anthology compilation.

10.   Sometimes (Felice Mancini / Henry Mancini) 2:53
"Sometimes" started out as a Christmas gift. Felice Mancini (daughter of Henry Mancini) wanted to give her parents something special for Christmas. She didn't want to just buy them something, but, instead, wanted to do something from her heart. She ended up writing a poem called "Sometimes," which reflected her honest and simple feelings for her friends and family. Henry Mancini (the composer of the Pink Panther Theme and the Peter Gunn Theme) was so taken by this lovely poem that he decided to put some music to it. After hearing that Karen and Richard were preparing to record a new album, Mancini called Jack Daugherty to offer the song to Carpenters. Richard loved the song and met with Mancini to let him know that he and Karen would record the song just as he sent it, vocal and piano.

The song is stark and simple, only one piano and one voice. This lovely composition opens with a one minute and twenty second piano solo by Richard, who is than joined by Karen with a moving and soulful vocal interpretation of Felice Mancini's beautiful poem.

Many Carpenters fans have used this song as a dedication to their friends and family. *"Sometimes, not often enough / We reflect upon the good things / And those thoughts always center / Around those we love..."*

A Song for You (click here to purchase)
Released: June 13, 1972
Producer: Jack Daugherty

Arrangements & Orchestration: Richard Carpenter
All Vocals: Karen Carpenter & Richard Carpenter
Drums: Karen Carpenter and Hal Blaine
Keyboards: Richard Carpenter, Tony Peluso
Guitar: Tony Peluso, Red Rhodes (steel guitar), Louie Shelton
Bass: Joe Osborn, Bob Messenger, Tony Peluso
Tenor Sax, Flute and Alto Flute: Bob Messenger
Bass Flute: Tim Weisberg
Oboe and English Horn: Earl Dumler
Bassoon: Norm Herzberg
Harp: Gayle Levant
Engineer: Ray Gerhardt
Assistant Engineer: Roger Young
Art Direction: Roland Young
Photography: Jim McCrary
Chart Positions: US #4/ UK #13/ Japan #5/ Australia #6/ Canada #5
Certifications: 3 x Multi-Platinum (RIAA)
Singles: Hurting Each Other/Maybe It's You, It's Going to Take Sometime/Flat Baroque, Goodbye to Love/Crystal Lullaby, Top of the World/Heather, I Won't Last a Day Without You/One Love (chart positions and release dates are listed in the song by song synopsis for this album)
Rick Henry's Rating: 9.7

After huge success with two consecutive albums, the pressure was on for Carpenters to produce a third consecutive smash hit. From the singles that had already been released, "Bless the Beasts and Children" (as a B-side), "Hurting Each Other" and "It's Going to Take Some Time," the public had a good idea that the upcoming album was going to be outstanding.

Karen and Richard kept a heavy schedule in 1972 with 174 concerts performed and six television appearances. Despite this crippling schedule they managed to put a few months' work into recording "A Song for You," their hallmark album that contains more hits for Carpenters than any of their other albums.

"A Song for You" introduced guitarist Tony Peluso to the world. Peluso's addition forever changed the sound of Carpenters music. This was best highlighted in the classic tune "Goodbye to Love," which features a fantastic fuzz guitar solo by Peluso. His influence on Carpenters music remained huge, especially on songs like "Jambalaya," "Please Mr. Postman," "Happy," "Only Yesterday," "Calling Occupants" and "Those Good Old Dreams."

Upon Richard Carpenter's insistence, this was the last album to give Jack Daugherty credit as producer. Richard hit the roof when a review in Cashbox Magazine started with the line, "Superb Jack Daugherty production." The fact that Daugherty was credited producer on the first four Carpenters albums really gnawed at Richard. In reality, the production credit belonged to Richard Carpenter, as he was the one who put the music together piece-by-piece from beginning to end. Daugherty scheduled appointments and made minor suggestions from time-to-time, but had very little to do with the creative development of the music or the choice of musicians. Herb Alpert and Jerry Moss dismissed Jack Daugherty in the fall of 1972. Daugherty took A&M to court claiming unfair dismissal. Daugherty lost this claim.

- **Note from Rick Henry:** *This is about as close to perfection that any pop group has ever achieved with an album. Each song on this album stands on its own. This is an album full of classics - one right after the other. It opens strongly with "A Song for You" and closes equally strongly with "Road Ode." The only song I may have omitted is "Piano Picker." Several fans like the tune because it somewhat tells the story of how Carpenters got their start playing music. Overall, though, as pleasant a little tune "Piano Picker" is, it just does not add to the overall strength to the album. For this one song, I refrain from giving "A Song for You" a 10 rating.*

1. <u>A Song for You (Leon Russell)</u> 4:42
    Leon Russell wrote and recorded this song for his first solo album, "Leon Russell" released in 1970. This song followed in the same dark and mournful tradition as "Rainy Days and Mondays" and "Superstar." By now

Carpenters had the dark and moody sound down to perfection.

Several legends of popular music have recorded this song, including: Cher, Bill Medley, Ray Charles, Andy Williams, Whitney Houston, Joe Cocker, Helen Reddy, Kenny Rankin, Celine Dion, Michael Buble, The Temptations and Neil Diamond, though the Carpenters' rendition remains the definitive recording. Richard's arrangement hits perfection and is absolutely amazing. His minimalist "less is more" arrangement put Karen's voice up front and center. Bob Messenger's steamy sax solo sends the song soaring to a higher plane. Karen Carpenter put every ounce of her heart and soul into an impeccable vocal performance. She sings with maturity, depth, sunlight and darkness. Karen utilizes the entire scope of her voice reaching deep into that basement voice (the lower, deep, dark portion of her voice) and then going into her beautifully, crystalline, higher register. Karen lives this song as she sings it. She makes the listener feel as if you are right there with her, experiencing every heart-wrenching moment of the song.

The combination of Richard's music and Karen's voice give this song that inescapable chill factor which is evident in almost all the Carpenters' music.

"A Song for You" had potential to be a hit single and may have possibly been released if the album didn't already have several hits from it. Instead, "A Song for You" has gone down in Carpenters history as one of their strongest album tracks.

- **Note from Rick Henry:** *"A Song for You" is an absolutely intense and thrilling song. I love Leon Russell, and I love Carpenters. You put them together and you have total magic as evidenced on the other Leon Russell tunes recorded by Carpenters, "Superstar" and "This Masquerade."*

2.   Top of the World (Richard Carpenter / John Bettis) 2:56

From the opening pedal steel guitar chords to Karen's sweet and lilting voice, "Top of the World" is an instant classic. It has an easygoing rhythm that can bring sunshine to the gloomiest of rainy days. Initially, Richard Carpenter and John Bettis viewed "Top of the World" as no more than a pleasant album track. The song had not been considered for release as a single. But, as time progressed, this little country tune (written by two kids from the suburbs of Southern California) seemed to grow in momentum. The first sign that the song had hit potential was the overwhelming response Carpenters would get when they performed the song in concert. The audience would jump to their feet and give the song a standing ovation every time they played it. The Japanese had already released the song as single where it rose to #21 and was certified gold. Then, Lynn Anderson had a hit with the song herself. She placed the song at #2 on the US country chart and #74 on the US pop chart in mid-1973. Most importantly, Carpenters version began to chart (in the US) based solely on radio airplay. Even though the song had not yet been released as a single, radio disc jockeys were getting heavy requests for the song, so stations around the states began playing it. Finally, due to huge demand, the song was released as a single in the US and worldwide. Its release, however, happened one year and three months after the release of its parent album. As a matter of fact, Carpenters had already released their next album, "Now and Then." Regardless, the single proved to be hugely profitable. It reached #1 in the US, as well as #5 UK, #1 Canada, #1 Australia, #3 Ireland, #14 Netherlands, #21 Japan and #38 Germany.

Before releasing "Top of the World" as a single, Carpenters took it back into the studio and rerecorded it. First, Karen's lead vocal was redone as Karen felt she had evolved quite a bit as a singer in the past year, and she thought she could do a better job with it. Richard was never happy with the steel guitar part, so Buddy Emmons was brought into the studio to play the steel guitar part that was initially done by Red Rhodes. Then, Tony Peluso added some of his own inimitable guitar work to the song. Finally, Richard Carpenter felt the song was ready to be unleashed onto the public. This version of the song was released on "The Singles 1969-1973" greatest hits compilation.

As the decades have passed, the legacy of "Top of the World" has grown. The song was used in a television commercial for Aquafina bottled water in 2004-2005 and was in heavy rotation for several months. It was used as the opening theme for the 2003 Japanese drama "Miseinen." It appeared in the 2010 soundtrack "Shrek Forever After" and was in a prominent scene in the 2012 movie "Dark Shadows."

3. Hurting Each Other (Gary Geld / Peter Udell) 2:46
    It is not known for certain who first recorded this tune, but the first group to have a hit with the song was the Guess Who (known at the time as Chad Allan and the Expressions). They took the song to #19 in Canada in early 1966. But it was the 1969 A&M recording by Ruby and the Romantics that caught Richard Carpenter's ear when he heard it on the radio - he was certain Ruby and the Romantics would turn this song into a hit. Richard was wrong in his prediction, but he never forgot the song and recorded it in late 1971.

    "Hurting Each Other" was the first, exciting, sneak peek into the not yet released "A Song for You" album (barring "Bless the Beasts and Children," which was released a few months earlier as the B-side of "Superstar"). Carpenters' rendition of the song retains some of Ruby and the Romantics bossa-nova feel working into a sheer power pop hook with a full range of intertwining instruments, interesting little sounds and nuances giving the song a sound and personality all its own.

    This time the song became a huge hit worldwide for Carpenters reaching #2 US, #2 Canada, #18 South Africa, #35 Australia and #56 Japan. Oddly enough, this song did not chart in the UK. "Hurting Each Other" was the Carpenters' sixth consecutive US million-selling

Gold certified single. Richard Carpenter commented that "Hurting Each Other" soared up the charts faster than any other Carpenters song.

Carpenters have gone on to record two more songs, which were previously recorded by Ruby and the Romantics: "Our Day Will Come" and "Your Baby Doesn't Love You Anymore."

4.   <u>It's Going to Take Sometime (Carole King / Toni Stern)</u>
2:55

Carole King and Carpenters made a perfect match, unfortunately, Carpenters recorded only one other Carole King penned song, "Our Day Will Come," which was part of the oldies medley on the "Now and Then" album.

Karen and Richard were at A&M working on their album "A Song for You" at the same time that Carole King was recording her album "Music," which was her follow-up to the mega-hit "Tapestry." Carole recorded for the Ode record label, which was a subsidiary of A&M. Richard happened to be there while Carole was recording her version of "It's Going to Take Sometime," and felt the song was a nice fit for Karen's voice and decided to record it. Carole King commented that Carpenters' recording made hers sound like a demo. Recording a Carole King song brought the Carpenters an air of "coolness" as she was extremely popular at the time.

Their eighth single to be released (and the second from "A Song for You") broke the Carpenters' string of six consecutive top three US hits. The song was still a big hit and received a huge amount of airplay but only reached US #12. It also charted at #13 Canada, #24 Australia and #48 Japan. This was the second consecutive Carpenters single to not chart in the UK. In hindsight Richard stated that this might not have been the best choice for a single release (I personally disagree).

5.   <u>Goodbye to Love (Richard Carpenter / John Bettis)</u> 3:50
"Goodbye to Love" is an important release for several reasons. This is their ninth single and is the first Carpenter/Bettis tune to be a single. Carpenter/Bettis had a few possibilities for singles earlier on with songs such as "All of My Life" and "Maybe It's You." Either the timing wasn't right, or the opportunity slipped away. "Goodbye to Love" was released one week before the album "A Song for You."

"Goodbye to Love" is also important for the fact that it put Carpenters back into the US Top 10 reaching #7, after the previous single "It's Going to Take Sometime" just missed the Top 10. The song also moved Carpenters back onto the singles chart in the UK, where both "Hurting Each Other" and "It's Going to Take Sometime" failed to chart.

Music fans and critics alike have described "Goodbye to Love," with its fuzz guitar solo, as being the model power ballad which influenced many others in the ensuing years and decades. Tony Peluso's guitar solo has been lauded by many in the music industry and has ended up on several lists of great guitar solos. On the other hand, some Carpenters fans fiercely opposed the song and felt Carpenters made a big mistake in recording a song that some described as "loud and harsh." Carpenters received some "hate mail" claiming that they had sold out and gone "hard rock." There were some Adult Contemporary radio stations that refused to play the song because of the guitar solo. Overall, the song received massive radio airplay and has gone on to become one of Carpenters' most loved and respected songs.

Richard wrote most of the melody while visiting London in the fall of 1971. The use of contrasting tones and long phrases makes it a very difficult song to sing. Karen handles the song with a natural ease and amazing control. Initially, the idea for the song came to Richard as he was watching an old 1940 Bing Crosby film called

"Rhythm on the River." The film was about a struggling songwriter who often mentioned his greatest composition "Goodbye to Love." The song is never heard in the movie - just mentioned several times. Richard immediately wrote the opening lyrics and melody, and then took it to John Bettis to complete the lyric.

Tony Peluso first crossed paths with Carpenters in 1971 when Mark Lindsay (lead singer of the band Paul Revere & The Raiders) was opening for Carpenters in concert. Peluso played guitar in the band Instant Joy, which was Lindsay's backing band. While working on "Goodbye to Love," Richard recalled Peluso's guitar work and decided there should be a fuzz guitar solo in it. Karen was given the duty of calling Tony. At first, Tony didn't believe that it was actually Karen Carpenter on the phone. In the studio, Tony first played something soft and tender, thinking that's what Richard would want for a Carpenters record. But Richard told Peluso to burn it up and let it soar into the stratosphere. The result was a huge success, and Tony ended up joining the Carpenters' recording and touring band. He stayed with them until the very end.

"Goodbye to Love" charted fairly well throughout the world reaching #4 Canada, #7 US, #9 UK, #12 Ireland, #25 Australia and #55 Japan.

- **Note from Rick Henry:** *"Goodbye to Love" is easily one of my ultimate favorite Carpenters tunes. It's the lyrics, it's Karen's voice... but mostly it's Tony Peluso's fuzz guitar solo... total genius.*

6.   <u>Intermission (Richard Carpenter)</u> :22
This 22-second a cappella piece is a humorous little break which was the closing on side one of the original 1972 vinyl record album release of the album "A Song for You." Richard wrote the lyrics and based the melody on "Crucifixus" by Antonio Lotti, a 17th/18th century Italian composer.

In a radio interview Richard had commented that "Intermission" was difficult to record. He also mentioned, humorously, that this is a prime example as to why he isn't a lyricist.

One longtime Carpenters fan has stated; "IT'S HUMOR at its best! Who else but Carpenters would do a musical little ditty like this in a million-part harmony? Plus, it ends the A-side of the vinyl album nicely. I thought it was clever, and it was brilliant."

7.   Bless the Beasts and Children (Berry DeVorzon /Perry Botkin, Jr) 3:07
By the time you get to this song, you are already very aware that "A Song for You" is a powerhouse album that is packed with hit after hit.
This was the first song anybody heard from the album. It was first heard in August 1971, when the film (of the same name) and the million-selling single "Superstar" (which featured "Bless the Beasts and Children" as its B-side) were released. This was 10 full months prior to the release of the album.

Stanley Kramer contacted Richard in early 1971 to discuss the possibility of recording the title song for his upcoming film. After hearing the demo, Richard agreed to record the song.

The Carpenters' soundtrack version differs slightly from the version featured on "A Song for You" and on the B-side of "Superstar." The soundtrack version opened with a vibraphone; the album and single version opens with an oboe.

"Bless the Beasts and Children" received so much airplay (as a B-side) that it made it onto the Billboard singles chart and reached #67. The song experienced further success when it was nominated for the 1972 Academy Award for Best Song but lost to Isaac Hayes' "Theme from Shaft." Karen and Richard appeared on the broadcast of the awards show to perform their nominated song.

Barry DeVorzon and Perry Botkins Jr. also wrote a song named "Cotton's Dream" for the "Bless the Beasts and Children" soundtrack. A few years later "Cotton's Dream" was used as the theme for the television soap opera "The Young and the Restless." Then, during the 1976 summer Olympics, the same song was used as the music for gymnast Nadia Comaneci. The song was then renamed "Nadia's Theme" and released as a single, which made the US Top 10.

- **Note from Rick Henry:** *Fantastically beautiful. This is the epitome of a Carpenters classic. It has all the elements: Karen's outstanding vocals, excellent musicianship, meaningful lyrics and that "chill factor." First class all the way.*

8. Flat Baroque (Richard Carpenter) 1:45
This sprite jazz-influenced instrumental dates back to 1966 while Richard was a music major at California State University, Long Beach. "Flat Baroque" is one of the tunes K&R recorded in 1967 for RCA Records.

Karen and Richard performed a slower version of this song on the "Your Navy Presents" radio show in early 1970.

Richard Carpenter slightly reworked the song for the 1972 recording, which features Richard on piano, Norm Herzberg on bassoon, and Karen spicing things up on the drums. Richard received a Grammy nomination for his arrangement of this song.

After completing the song Norm Herzberg commented, "This isn't exactly what I had in mind when I left the house this morning."

9. Piano Picker (Randy Edelman) 1:59
This song seems almost autobiographical of Richard's life that you'd think he wrote it himself. Instead, Randy Edelman, who also wrote "I Can't Make Music" from the "Now & Then" album and "You" from "A Kind of Hush"

wrote it. Edelman toured with Carpenters in 1971. He's also well-known for writing the Barry Manilow hit "Weekend in New England."

Some fans especially enjoy this song because they feel it gives them an insight into Richard's beginnings with music and his joy in creating it.

10. <u>I Won't Last a Day Without You (Paul Williams / Roger Nichols)</u> 3:46

By popular demand "I Won't Last a Day Without You" was released as a single on March 25, 1974. This was nearly two years after the album was released and was the sixth song from the album to make the US charts. This once again proved the durability of the album "A Song for You." The song reached #11 in the US, #7 in Canada, #40 in Japan, #63 in Australia and UK #32 (it had previously reached UK #9 in 1972 as a double A-side with "Goodbye To Love"). The song was also certified Gold in Japan and won Japan's World Disc Grand Prix award for Single of the Year.

Before releasing the song as a single, Carpenters took the song back into the studio. They rerecorded and remixed a few parts adding a nice touch with some new guitar parts by Tony Peluso.

Several others have recorded the song, including Barbra Streisand, Diana Ross, Maureen McGovern, and Al Wilson (as part of a medley).

11. <u>Crystal Lullaby (Richard Carpenter / John Bettis)</u> 3:58

This dreamy ballad features both Karen and Richard sharing lead vocals and was used as the B-side for the mega-hit "Goodbye to Love."

Richard and John wrote "Crystal Lullaby" in 1968, and is the last of the Spectrum-era tunes included on any Carpenters albums. Carpenters recorded a total of eight Spectrum songs which include "Turn Away," "All I Can Do," "Maybe It's You," Crescent

Noon," "Mr. Guder," "Another Song," "Saturday" and "Crystal Lullaby."

12. Road Ode (Gary Sims / Danny Woodhams) 3:50
"Road Ode" closes this album just as strong as it opens. On this song, Karen's voice is filled with longing and passion and enveloped in rich and dark soulful tones. She seems to maintain a certain authority about the subject of living life on the road during a long concert tour. During this time period Carpenters were performing over 200 concerts per year.

The song's authors, Gary Sims (bassist) and Danny Woodhams (guitar), were both longtime members of Carpenters' road band. They both knew and understood the hardships of living life on the road and moving from one city to another day after day.

Fans consider this to be one of Carpenters' very best album tracks for many reasons, but are particularly drawn to it for its personal nature. Karen sings the lines of this song with such believability because she had been living life on the road for almost two years.

- **Note from Rick Henry:** *This is my favorite song from this album. Karen sings this song from the heart. She's singing from experience here. I love the story the song tells of a "rock star" on the road.*

13. A Song for You (Reprise) (Leon Russell) :53
With heavy echo added, this 53-second reprise is a delightful reminder of what a wonderful album this is from beginning to end. Since Karen's passing, the haunting lyrics of this reprise – fading away, are extremely poignant and touching. *"And when my life is over remember when we were together..."*

Carpenters enjoyed the theme of bookending their albums with a similar song or a reprise of a song at the beginning and end of their albums. The first time they did this was with their debut album "Offering" (aka "Ticket to Ride") when they opened and closed the album with the bookend pieces "Invocation" and "Benediction." In 1973, they did it again on the B-side of their "Now & Then" album, which opened with "Yesterday Once More," followed by the "Oldies Medley" and closed with an echoic reprise of "Yesterday Once More." Finally, their majestic 1975 album "Horizon" opened and closed with the mesmerizing bookend pieces "Aurora" and "Eventide."

Now & Then (click here to purchase)
Released: May 9, 1973
Producer: Richard and Karen Carpenter
Arrangements & Orchestration: Richard Carpenter
All Vocals: Karen Carpenter & Richard Carpenter
Drums: Karen Carpenter (except on "Jambalaya"), Hal Blaine ("Jambalaya")
Keyboards: Richard Carpenter
Guitar: Tony Peluso (lead and rhythm guitar), Gary Sims (rhythm guitar), Buddy Emmons (steel guitar), Jay Dee Maness (steel guitar)
Bass: Joe Osborne
Tenor Sax and Flute: Bob Messenger
Baritone Saxophone: Doug Strawn
Oboe, Bass Oboe and English Horn: Earl Dumler
Recorder: Tom Scott
Harp: Gayle Levant
Harmonica: Tommy Morgan
Backing Vocals on "Sing": The Jimmy Joyce Singing Chorus
Disc Jockey on Oldies Medley: Tony Peluso
Engineer: Ray Gerhardt
Assistant Engineer: Roger Young
Mastering Engineer: Bernie Grundman
Art Direction: Roland Young
Photography: Jim McCrary (front cover)
Illustrations: Design Maru (front cover), Len Freas (inside cover)
Special Thanks: Ron Gorow
Chart Positions: US #2/ UK #2/ Japan #1/ Australia #3/ Canada #2/ Netherlands #2/ Norway #12
Certifications: 2 x Multi-Platinum (US - RIAA) / Gold (UK)
Singles: Sing / Druscilla Penny, Yesterday Once More / Road Ode, Jambalaya / Mr. Guder (UK release) (chart positions and

release dates are listed in the song by song synopsis from this album)
Rick Henry's Rating: 9.4

This album was released on May 9, 1973. "Now & Then" was a huge hit worldwide. It was their best-selling studio album internationally (with "Horizon" their second best-selling). This was the first album to list Richard and Karen Carpenter as the producers. "Now & Then" was one of two albums to feature Karen playing drums on all the tracks (with the exception of "Jambalaya"), the other album being 1969's "Offering/Ticket to Ride."

Carpenters once again displayed a growth and maturity with adeptness to a variation of styles of music. Karen shines vocally on "This Masquerade," while the group rocks on their take of the Beach Boys' classic "Fun, Fun, Fun." "Now & Then" was the album released just before the classic, multi-million selling greatest hits package titled "Singles 1969-1973."

Due to a heavy touring schedule and the demand to get an album out as soon as possible, there was only one Richard Carpenter/John Bettis song on the album "Yesterday Once More," which turned out to be their second biggest-selling single worldwide (the first is "Please Mr. Postman").

The album was considered somewhat a theme album in that Side One was considered the "Now" side with new songs such as "This Masquerade," "I Can't Make Music" and "Sing" and Side Two was the "Then" side with the "Oldies Medley." Side two opened with "Yesterday Once More," a wistful song telling the story of the old songs on the radio. The song was followed by the 14 ½ minute long "Oldies Medley." Many fans considered this to be a highlight of the album, while other fans wished that full-length songs of "Our Day Will Come," "Johnny Angel," "The End of the World," "Da Doo Ron Ron" and "One Fine Day" were in place instead of the medley.

While Richard was speaking to mom Carpenter about the album, she suggested the title "Now & Then" to him.

Carpenters guitarist, Tony Peluso, is heard throughout the "Oldies Medley" as a radio disc jockey. Mark Rudolph, a cousin of the Carpenters, can be heard on the "Guess the Golden Goodies Group Contest," as the listener who calls in.

The "Now & Then" album cover has been featured in several album cover books, particularly for its three-panel, gatefold layout. The cover opens up to a panoramic view of Karen and Richard in (Richard's) red Ferrari.

- **Note from Rick Henry:** *I gave this album a 9.4 rating for a few factors. As a whole this is a fantastic album. "This Masquerade" alone is worth the price of the album. Fortunately, there are other great tunes, such as "I Can't Make Music" and "Yesterday Once More." I feel that as well-loved as "Sing" was, the album would have been stronger had the song been replaced with another dark ballad along the lines of "This Masquerade." Even Richard Carpenter has said he should have spent more time recording songs like "This Masquerade" instead of "Sing." That being said, I still like the song "Sing," but it's not a favorite. Although I do love the "Oldies Medley," I am one of those who would have preferred full-length versions of the better songs in the medley without any interruption of the disc jockey. Despite these few things, I love "Now & Then" and consider it to be one of my favorite Carpenters albums.*

1. Sing (Joe Raposo) 3:18
    Joe Raposo, a staff songwriter for the popular PBS children's television series "Sesame Street," wrote "Sing." Bob McGrath, with the Muppets and Big Bird, usually performed the song on the show.

    Joe Raposo wrote the song to accompany a short film of children playing during the 1971 season of "Sesame Street." Bob Cranshaw, a well-known bass player and also member of the Sesame Street band, introduced "Sing" to Peggy Lee. It was Lee's version that was heard by Carpenters, who then called Joe Raposo to ask permission to record "Sing."

Before Carpenters did their recording, Barbra Streisand released a somewhat sultry, serious, ballad version of the song which reached #28 on the US Adult Contemporary chart. But it was Carpenters who turned this song into a multi-million selling, worldwide hit. "Sing" was played on radio stations around the world. Many fans have referred to this song as having a universal charm. Carpenters discovered the song in late 1972, while taping a guest appearance on the TV Special "Robert Young with the Young."

"Sing" brought Carpenters back into the US Top Three after 1972's "It's Going to Take Sometime" #12 and "Goodbye to Love" #7. "Sing" also received Gold status for selling over a million copies (which by today's standards would have been certified platinum). The Jimmy Joyce Children's Chorus joined Karen and Richard on vocals.

Critics panned the song heavily calling it trite and lacking in substance. Regardless, the music industry loved the song, and it received two Grammy award nominations, one for Richard's arrangement and the other for Best Pop Vocal Performance.

Two other versions of the song exist, including a live version in which Karen sings part of the song in Japanese. This can be found on the "Live in Japan" album. The other version of the song is sung in both Spanish and English and is called "Canta/Sing," which can be found on the box set "From the Top." The Spanish lyric was recorded a few months after the original in response to requests from affiliates from Spanish-speaking countries.

2. This Masquerade (Leon Russell) 4:50
Although the Carpenters never released "This Masquerade" as an A-side single, it is widely known as a Carpenters classic. The song has ended up on countless

Carpenters compilations, including: "Yesterday Once More," "Interpretations," "Treasures," "From the Top," "Love Songs," "Gold: 35th Anniversary Edition," "The Ultimate Collection," "40/40" and several others.

Leon Russell wrote and originally recorded this song for his 1972 album "Carney" which also includes his Top 10 hit "Tight Rope." Russell also wrote "A Song for You" and "Superstar."

Richard Carpenter took the song and transformed it into an elegant, cocktail-lounge tune of superior quality. Karen Carpenter's vocal is deep, dark and smoky. Many consider this to be one of her finest performances. At the age of twenty-three, Karen sings with a graceful maturity and depth far beyond her youthful age. Displaying her ability as a multi-talented musician, Karen plays the drums on this song to perfection, showing off her specialty in understated, yet complex, jazz patterns. Bob Messenger displays his finesse with the saxophone in a hot and steamy sax solo (much like his sax solo on "A Song for You").

Many Carpenters fans considered the song strong enough to be a single and rate this song amongst their very best.

Along with being a highlight track from "Now & Then," "This Masquerade" was used as the B-side to the 1974-75 worldwide #1 hit single "Please Mr. Postman."

R&B/Jazz singer/guitarist George Benson recorded an equally outstanding version of the song in 1976 and took it all the way into the US Top 10.

- **Note from Rick Henry:** *"This Masquerade" ranks within my Top 10 favorite Carpenters tunes. They should have recorded more songs like this one. It is absolutely one of their finest recordings all the way around. It has a dark and mysterious mood about it. Karen sings this one to perfection. Outstanding!*

3. <u>Heather (Johnny Pearson)</u> 2:49
   This ethereal instrumental was written in 1968 by John Pearson, and is a vehicle to showcase Richard's keyboard finesse. "Heather" was used as the B-side of the 1973 #1 hit "Top of the World."

   Johnny Pearson is a British pianist and composer. He led the Top of the Pops Orchestra from 1966 until 1981. He's worked with several leading British musicians, such as Cilia Black, Dusty Springfield and John Paul Jones.

   Johnny Pearson first collaborated with Carpenters when he helped in producing their 1971 "Live at the BBC" concert film.

   "Heather" was originally called "Autumn Reverie" and was featured on Johnny Pearson's 1968 album "Gentle Sounds." Richard Carpenter first heard the song when it was being used as background music for a Geritol television commercial in the US. Richard immediately loved the song and contacted Pearson to get permission to record it for "Now & Then." John Bettis (Carpenters lyricist) came up with the name "Heather."

4. <u>Jambalaya (On the Bayou) (Hank Williams)</u> 3:40
   Bluegrass Country music legend, Hank Williams Sr., wrote and introduced this song in 1952, and it reached # 1 on the country music charts as well as # 20 on the US pop charts. That same year Jo Stafford (princess of standards, who had 78 hits from 1944 to 1957) took the song to # 3. Since then several others have recorded and charted with the song, including Fats Domino who reached US # 30 and UK # 41 in 1962. The Blue Ridge Rangers (formed by John Fogerty who was previously the singer, songwriter and guitarist of Creedence Clearwater Revival) had a hit with the song in 1973 reaching US # 16.

   Despite all the major success this song has achieved, Carpenters have had the biggest hit with it worldwide. In 1974, they took the song to #12 in the UK, #12 in

Ireland, #50 in Germany, #95 in Australia, #8 in Austria, #13 in Belgium and #28 in Japan (also certified GOLD in Japan). In Holland the song became their biggest hit reaching #3. Although "Jambalaya" received quite a bit of radio airplay, it was never released as a single in the US. Some speculate it could have been a Top Three US hit.

Carpenters originally recorded the rhythm track for this song in 1972, but dismissed it as they worked on other projects such as touring and doing television appearances. In early 1973, while working on the "Now & Then" album, they finished the song due to a lack of time to write new tunes.

- **Note from Rick Henry:** *Although I do not rate this as one of Carpenters' finest works, it is still one of my favorite Carpenters tunes. I have always been attracted to upbeat, feel-good songs, and this is one such song. I just love it and never tire of it.*

5. <u>I Can't Make Music (Randy Edelman)</u> 3:17
Songwriter Randy Edelman performed this song while opening for Carpenters in concert. Richard loved Edelman's song immediately and felt it was perfect for Karen and decided to record it. "I Can't Make Music" is one of the most moving and mysterious songs in the Carpenters entire library of recorded music. Adding to the mysteriously, dark feel is the unusual violin/harmonica duet at the end of the song. Karen sings it as if she is truly singing about herself. Her dark, deep, mournful voice digs into your soul and captures you at your most vulnerable moments. You can feel every bit of emotion represented in Karen's voice. "I Can't Make Music" is a somber piece of perfection in a song.

Edelman also wrote the songs "Piano Picker" from the album "A Song for You" and "You" from "A Kind of Hush."

Although rarely used in compilations, "I Can't Make

Music" remains a huge favorite amongst Carpenters fans.

- **Note from Rick Henry:** *This is my favorite song from "Now & Then." The lyrics are emotive, and Karen's voice shines throughout. This lands in my Top Five Carpenters songs.*

6. Yesterday Once More (Richard Carpenter / John Bettis)
3:50

"When I was young, I'd listen to the radio..."
On the original vinyl release of "Now & Then," "Yesterday Once More" opened side two and segued into the "Oldies Medley." Side two of the album was considered the "Then" portion featuring "Yesterday Once More," a song paying homage to the warm feeling of hearing the oldies of the previous decade, followed by a medley of oldies from the early 60's. Karen's mournful and sweet, honey-toned voice lent itself perfectly to the nostalgic feel of the song.

During this time period (1973) the US was experiencing a big resurgence of oldies from the 1950's and 60's. It wasn't just the music but also clothing fashions and televisions shows such as "Happy Days" that helped this resurgence. Richard Carpenter felt it fitting that he and Bettis write a song in tribute to the Golden Oldies. Originally, "Yesterday Once More" was to include a verse with titles of songs from the sixties. Karen Carpenter commented that she hated the idea. This idea was quickly abandoned as trite and unworkable. With "Yesterday Once More," Richard and John captured the warmth and nostalgia of listening to those oldies from the early 60's. The chorus *"Every sha la la la"* and *"Every wo wo wo"* were dummy lyrics used to sing along during the song writing process. It was assumed that real words would replace the dummy lines. As the song progressed both Richard and John decided the dummy verses sounded good and kept them in.

"Yesterday Once More" was released as a single on May 16, 1973, just two weeks after the release of "Now &

Then." The song became the Carpenters' second biggest hit worldwide reaching #2 in both the US and UK, #1 in Canada, #5 in Japan, #6 Norway, Netherlands #7, #8 Ireland, #9 in Australia, #21 Germany. It was also certified Gold in the US, UK, and Japan.

7. The Oldies Medley (Various) 14:15
The classic "Yesterday Once More" fades out with the sounds of a roaring motorcycle, which works neatly into the thrilling OLDIES MEDLEY. The medley is set-up like an oldies, radio broadcast complete with a groovin' disc jockey enthusiastically performed by Carpenters guitarist extraordinaire Tony Peluso.

The medley starts out with FUN, FUN, FUN, the Beach Boys' 1964 top five hit. Richard provides a strong lead vocal while Karen moves right in with her ever-sweet and soulful back-up and harmony vocals.

THE END OF THE WORLD Clocking in at two minutes and twenty five seconds this song is long enough to be an individual track. It was originally recorded in 1963 by Skeeter Davis. Skeeter broke records with this song reaching not only #1 on the US pop charts, but also #1 on the adult contemporary chart, #2 on the country and western chart, and #4 on the R&B chart. In 1963, Karen (13 years old) and Richard (17 years old) performed in a local talent show in one of the parks in Downey, CA. Richard played the "Theme From Exodus," and then Karen joined him and sang "The End of the World" in her high voice (she hadn't yet developed her lower register). Even in 1963 Karen and Richard were capturing the attention of those who listened.

Carpenters fans consider "The End of the World" as one of their favorites from the medley.

DA DOO RON RON In 1973, Carpenters did their own superb, upbeat recording of this 1963 classic, including a great sax solo by Bob Messenger and aggressive guitar works by Tony Peluso. "Da Doo Ron Ron," written by Jeff Barry, Ellie Greenwich and Phil Spector, was first a top 3 hit in 1963 for the female vocal group The Crystals. The Crystals were discovered by Phil Spector and also reached the top ten with "He's a Rebel" and "Then He Kissed Me." Also, in 1977, Shaun Cassidy topped the charts with the song, changing the lyric to "Da Doo Ron Ron (When She Walked Me Home)." "Da Doo Ron Ron" is one of Richard's favorite, Phil Spector-produced Crystals hits. While Carpenters were recording the song, Phil Spector happened to be at A&M studios. He peeked into the studio and complimented the band on the recording.

DEAD MAN'S CURVE Hot rod racing equals street car crash. While the Carpenters recorded this song, Richard was wearing a cast due to a motorcycle accident he was in earlier in the year. Richard could really relate to the song. Richard takes the lead here and hits a homerun. The song includes the sounds of screeching wheels and breaking glass. It was so far removed from anything else the Carpenters had recorded up to this point. Richard said that his love of Spike Jones influenced the sound effects used in this song. Richard had a hard time keeping a straight face while he recited the spoken part of the song starting out *"Well, Doc, the last thing I remember, I started to swerve..."* Everybody in the studio was cracking up, from the engineers to Karen. A fun time was had while recording the song.

"Dead Man's Curve" was recorded by surf-rock duo Jan & Dean in 1964 and reached the Top 10. Jan & Dean also had hits with "Surf City" and "Little Old Lady From Pasadena."

JOHNNY ANGEL From the shattering glass of "Dead Man's Curve" comes the heavenly-chiming of "Johnny Angel" which leads to Karen's multi-tracked harmony vocals. What a beautiful sound the Carpenters created with this song. The song is perfectly suited to Karen's deep, honey-toned vocals. Fans consider this a highlight of the entire oldies medley, and many have often wished Carpenters would have recorded a full length version of the song.

"Johnny Angel" was originally a 1962 #1 hit for Shelley Fabares. Shelley's television credits include regular roles on "One Day at a Time" and "Coach." She also appeared in three Elvis Presley movies. Though, she is best remembered for her role as Mary Stone on television's "Donna Reed Show."

THE NIGHT HAS A THOUSAND EYES Many fans consider this to be one of Richard's best vocals. This quick-moving, upbeat song really hits its stride when Karen joins in with harmony vocals on the infectious chorus. Being a fan of Bobby Vee's records, Richard has claimed he likes the chord changes in "The Night Has a Thousand Eyes."

"Thousand Eyes" was a Top Three hit in 1962-63 for Bobby Vee, who also scored hits with "Devil or Angel", "Rubber Ball", "Take Good Care of My Baby" and "Run to Him."

OUR DAY WILL COME This song seems to be the favorite of the entire oldies medley. Richard Carpenter comments that this is one of Karen's finest vocals ever. Karen's performance is full-bodied, deep, rich, and sensuous. From the very beginning it was evident that "Our Day Will Come" was to be included in the medley. In 1963 Ruby And The Romantics (who also recorded "Hurting Each Other" and "Your Baby Doesn't Love You Anymore") reached #1 with "Our Day Will Come."

In the OLDIES MEDLEY between "The Night Has a Thousand Eyes" and "Our Day Will Come," disc jockey Tony Peluso asks the question, "Mark Rudolph! Can you give me the identity of our GOLDEN MYSTERY GROUP?" Mark Rudolph answers, "Yeah, the Four Seasons" (which is the wrong answer). Frankie Valli did, however, end up recording "Our Day Will Come" in 1975, and reached the Top 15 with it.

ONE FINE DAY The Carpenters' rendition of this Carole

King/Gerry Goffin penned classic is upbeat and playful and presents a carefree, perfect pop-vocal by Karen. Originally a Top Five hit in 1963 for the Chiffons, Carole King herself reached US #12 in 1980 with the song.

8.   Yesterday Once More (Reprise)(Richard Carpenter/John Bettis) :58

Heavy on echo and sound effects, this 58- second reprise of the golden Carpenters classic neatly brings the high-spirited OLDIES MEDLEY to a close. And, it leaves the listener almost breathless and wanting to hear the entire album all over again.

- **Note from Rick Henry:** *During this time period, I would listen to Carpenters with the headphones on. I didn't want to miss any single sound; I wanted to hear it all. Karen's voice and each and every instrument sounded fresh and crisp and brand new every time I'd listen.*

> *It was songs of love that*
> *I would sing to then,*
> *And I'd memorize each word.*
> *Those old melodies*
> *Still sound so good to me*
> *As they melt the years away.*

Horizon (click here to purchase)
Released: June 6, 1975
Producer: Richard Carpenter
Associate Producer: Karen Carpenter
Arrangements & Orchestration: Richard Carpenter
All Vocals: Karen Carpenter & Richard Carpenter
Drums: Karen Carpenter and Jim Gordon
Keyboards: Richard Carpenter
Guitar: Tony Peluso
Steel Guitar: Thad Maxwell and Red Rhodes
Bass: Joe Osborn
Tenor Sax: Bob Messenger
Baritone Sax: Doug Strawn
Oboe and English Horn: Earl Dumler
Harmonica: Tom Morgan
Harp: Gayle Levant

Engineer: Roger Young and Ray Gerhardt
Assistant Engineer: Dave Iveland
Mastering Engineer: Bernie Grundman
Art Direction: Roland Young
Photography: Ed Caraeff
Special Thanks: Ron Gorow
Special Credits for "I Can Dream Can't I" (see below in the description of the song)
Chart Positions: US #13/ UK #1/ Japan #1/ Australia #21/ Canada #4/ New Zealand #3/ Norway #5/ Germany #42/ Netherlands #21
Certifications: Platinum (US), Gold (UK, Japan and Canada)
Singles: Please Mr. Postman/This Masquerade, Only Yesterday/Happy, Solitaire/Love Me for What I Am
Rick Henry's Rating: 10

Horizon is the album that most die-hard Carpenters fans claim to be their favorite of all Carpenters releases. Released on June 6, 1975, critics hail this to be the most sophisticated Carpenters album to date. The album is a technological triumph. It was recorded at A&M Records, mainly in Studio D, using state-of-the-art 24-track recording technology, 30 Dolby, and recorded at 30 inches per second to create the cleanest and clearest sound possible.

The Carpenters took the patience to spend a good amount of time and many long hours experimenting with different sounds, techniques and effects. One of the most astonishing techniques used on the album is the multitude of separate mikings. Every single instrument and voice has its own microphone. This helped to create a broad, full sound. The drums were recorded on four separate tracks, one for the kick, one for the snare and one each for the left and right tom-toms. On the song "Only Yesterday," a tape delay is used on the saxophone - this effect accents the instrument and lifts it above the canvas and gives it an extra dimension.

"Horizon" was the Carpenters' sixth studio album. After five consecutive albums peaking inside the US Top Five, "Horizon" broke this run by reaching US # 13. The album has been certified PLATINUM by the RIAA for selling over a million copies and most likely will soon be certified DOUBLE

PLATINUM. Although "Horizon" showed hints of Carpenters sales slowing up in the US, they were bigger than ever around the world. "Horizon" was one of their biggest, worldwide sellers reaching # 1 in both Japan and England.

Richard Carpenter stated that his goal was to produce an album where every song could be a single. With "Horizon," he achieved this goal, as each song on this album could have easily been a hit in 1975.

Jerry Moss (the "M" in A&M Records) sent Richard a letter congratulating him on his production of "Horizon." This was a big deal to both Karen and Richard as Moss rarely showed much appreciation for Carpenters. During the recording of "Horizon," Moss visited Carpenters in the studio and recognized what a thrill it was to have a voice like Karen Carpenter's recording for A&M.

In the Ray Coleman book, The Carpenters: The Untold Story, it is stated that some felt "Horizon" showed a growth of experimental, ground-breaking qualities comparable to the Beatles' "Sgt. Peppers." Coleman also stated that "Horizon" is a classy work which has stood the test of time.

- **Note from Rick Henry:** *"Horizon" is easily my favorite of all Carpenters albums. The sound is well thought out and a huge step forward in the technological side of the musical production. I really enjoy the somber mood of the songs and the mature nature of the album overall. What I find most amazing about "Horizon" is how perfectly the vocals were melded together. Carpenters have always excelled in their vocal performances, but with "Horizon" Richard Carpenter took the production and the layering of vocals to a new height. "Horizon" will always be my favorite Carpenters album.*

1. Aurora (Richard Carpenter / John Bettis) 1:32
    "Morning opens quietly, a shadow vision over me..."
    Horizon opens and closes with a pair of distant, yet warmly familiar bookend songs: "Aurora" and "Eventide." Each song is identical in its somber mood

with a chilling sense of sunrise and sunset. "Aurora" sets the atmosphere of the album, giving the listener a hint of the melancholy moods awaiting.

2. <u>Only Yesterday (Richard Carpenter / John Bettis)</u> 4:11
From "Aurora," the album moves right on to "Only Yesterday," which many consider to be the album's strongest track. Written by Richard Carpenter and lyricist John Bettis, the song was a huge hit worldwide. Believing the song would not be a hit, Carpenter and Bettis lost a one-thousand dollar bet to their recording engineer Roger Young. Since the melody was upbeat, Richard asked Bettis to make sure the lyrics were not completely sad, so the outlook of the song changes midstream. It goes from dark and mournful to bright and propulsive. Bettis described "Only Yesterday" as, "a manipulated, positive song." The song has an impressive "wall of sound" with each instrument clearly recognizable. It has the feel of the sixties with castanets and chimes and the technology of the 70's with electric guitar chords and soulful saxophone progressions. Even with all the cutting edge technology, it's Karen's voice that remains the focal point. She opens with a haunting Low E Flat and moves gracefully through the range of the song and her voice with ease. "Only Yesterday" is two songs in one, with a lush ballad verse which effectively gives way to an up-tempo progressive pop chorus.

Parts of the music video for the song were filmed at Huntington Library Gardens in San Marino, CA.

Richard Carpenter has described this song as being "a complicated arrangement." They put a good amount of work into every aspect of the song to make it work. The opening kick drum and snare (which is now considered a classic song opening by Carpenters fans) was performed by Jim Gordon and really gets the song moving. Tony Peluso adds several different intricate guitar chords and riffs throughout the song. It's a very eclectically-electric song.

"Only Yesterday" was released in the US on March 14, 1975, and was Carpenters' last Top 10 hit in the US. The song did extremely well throughout the world, reaching US #4, UK #7, Canada #2, Germany #43, Ireland #5, New Zealand #10 and Japan #12. The song was also certified Gold in Japan and won the prestigious Japanese GRAND PRIX award in 1975.

Carpenters superfan, Tim (aka Martini's Musings), has said the song is, "rather intricate, the many parts being sung - lots and lots of great harmony. And, it's executed flawlessly."

- **Note from Rick Henry:** *I would have to say, ultimately, this is my favorite of all Carpenters songs. It's that opening kick drum by Jim Gordon, Tony Peluso's ever-fantastic guitar work, John Bettis' lyrics, Richard Carpenter's seamless arrangement, the perfectly multi-layered vocals and Karen's basement voice. I love the way Karen's and Richard's voices weave in-and-out of each other in the backing and harmony vocals. It's all there, every single element of a great Carpenters tune – nothing is missing.*

  This is the ultimate pop song. It has that great, wall of sound. There's a lot going on in this song and each instrument is carefully placed and is clearly distinguishable. Why Richard did not receive at least a Grammy award nomination for this arrangement is beyond me.

  "You were the dawn breaking the night/ The promise of morning light/ Filling the world, surrounding me...."

3. Desperado (Don Henley / Glen Frey) 3:38
    This song received a good amount of attention from the critics stating this was a logical choice for release as a single. The intensely, emotional song received rave reviews. It was an instant favorite amongst fans and critics alike. Karen wrung out every bit of her soul as she brought this song alive. She sang it like she really

meant it. Tommy Morgan's harmonica accents the overall aura of the song; his haunting performance establishes the song's melancholy mood.

"Desperado" was originally recorded by the Eagles in 1973, and was the centerpiece of their classic, cowboy-themed album also named "Desperado." Several others have recorded this song including Linda Ronstadt, Bonnie Raitt, Kenny Rogers, Clint Black, Johnny Cash and Neil Diamond.

A&M Records decided against releasing Carpenters' version as a single, due to the fact that it had been receiving radio airplay for both Eagles and Linda Ronstadt. Many fans consider this to be a "missed opportunity."

- **Note from Rick Henry:** *Again, this is amongst my ultimate favorites by Carpenters. I love the sleek and sophisticated sound. "Desperado," without a doubt, contains that "chill factor." I feel this is one of Karen's finest vocals ever - deep, rich, pure, strong and soulful. Karen was truly at her vocal best when recording the fabulous album "Horizon."*

4. Please Mr. Postman (Georgia Dobbins / William Garrett / Freddie Gorman / Brain Holland / Robert Bateman) 2:53
    "Please Mr. Postman" was never meant to be anything more than a feel-good pop song, and what a great pop song it was. Carpenters recorded and released this song in late 1974 (a full seven months before "Horizon" was released). For its inclusion on "Horizon," Richard Carpenter remixed the song and gave it a glossier sheen than what was on the single.

    While recording the song some of the engineers and musicians thought Karen and Richard were "nuts" to even consider it, but the duo got the last laugh when it became a worldwide #1 smash.

"Please Mr. Postman" was the album's biggest hit single and also Carpenters' biggest hit worldwide. It reached # 1 in the US, Australia, Canada and South Africa, as well as reaching # 2 in the UK and Canada. It also reached #4 New Zealand, #5 Switzerland, #10 Germany, #11 Japan and #29 Netherlands. This driving, rhythm-based tune features Karen on drums and a great Tony Peluso guitar solo.

The music video for the song was filmed at Disneyland in Anaheim, CA. Karen and Richard are treated like VIP's in the theme park, as they are escorted by Disney dignitaries such as Goofy, Donald Duck and Mickey Mouse. The video perfectly captures the feel-good feel of the song.

Richard Carpenter has always loved this song (most predominantly the Beatles' recording) and had wanted to record the song for quite some time.

"Please Mr. Postman" is one of a handful of songs to be a US #1 hit more than once. It reached #1 first in 1961 for the female, Motown vocal group the Marvelettes. The song also gained further acclaim when the Beatles included it on their 1963 album "With the Beatles."

- **Note from Rick Henry:** *I love this song; always have, always will.*

5. I Can Dream Can't I? (Sammy Fain / Irving Kahal) 4:59
    In the liner notes for the album "Horizon," this song contains its own separate personnel credits. The credits are as follows:
    Arranged by Billy May and Richard Carpenter
    Orchestrated by Billy May
    Bass: Joe Mondragon
    Drums: Alvin Stoller
    Keyboards: Pete Jolly
    Vibes: Frank Flynn
    Guitar: Bob Bain
    Background Vocals: Jackie Ward, Mitch Gordon, John Bahler and Gene Merlino

Considered by many to be a highlight of the album, "I Can Dream Can't I?" is an atmospheric interpretation of the 1949 Andrews Sisters hit. To maintain an authentic quality, Karen and Richard hired veteran, Billy May, to orchestrate the song. May has worked with legends, such as Frank Sinatra and Nat King Cole. The song features the Billy May Orchestra, which adds to the authenticity of the overall sound. One gets the mental image of Karen dressed in a formal gown, her hair perfectly coifed as she fronts a fabulous 40's-style big band to perform the dreamy number.

"I Can Dream Can't I?" was written and published in 1938 for the musical "Right This Way," which was a commercial flop. Later in the year, Tommy Dorsey recorded the song and had a hit with it. It wasn't until 1949 that the song reached national acclaim when the Andrews Sisters hit #1 with the song. Although Carpenters never released it as a single, their rendition has received a fair amount of radio airplay on nostalgic radio stations as well as jazz, easy listening, adult contemporary and standards radio.

John Bahler is in the chorus of background singers. Bahler and his brother Tom (whom Karen dated) hired Karen and Richard in early 1969 to promote the Ford Motor Company and most prominently the new car, the Maverick. Alvin Stoller plays drums on this track; he is best known for his work in the 1940's and 50's with legendary big bands such as Tommy Dorsey, Harry James and Benny Goodman. Pete Jolly is a jazz keyboardist whose composition "Little Bird" was nominated for a 1963 Grammy Award. Jolly has also done extensive work recording television theme songs such as "I Spy," "Love Boat," "MASH," "Get Smart," "Mannix," "Dallas" and many others.

A bit on the songwriters: Sammy Fain was inducted into the Songwriters Hall of Fame in 1972 and has won two Academy Awards for "Secret Love" from Calamity Jane (1954) and "Love Is a Many-Splendored Thing" from the movie of the same name (1955). Irving Kahal's most notable tune is "You Brought a New Kind of Love to Me" which he wrote with Pierre Norman. The song was made popular by Maurice Chavalier in the movie "The Big Pond" (1930). Frank Sinatra also recorded the song.

6. Solitaire (Neil Sedaka / Phil Cody) 4:40
    Neil Sedaka and Phil Cody wrote "Solitaire" which was the third single from "Horizon." The exuberance of the strings, Richard's subtle keyboard and Karen's deep, full-bodied voice give this song that chill factor that Richard looked for in a song. Many Carpenters fans consider this to be one of Karen's most intense and finest readings. Some even go so far as to say this is Karen's very best vocal performance.

    Richard Carpenter has commented that Karen never liked the song. Fans have speculated as to the reason why Karen never cared for this spectacular song; some theorize it could be due to the fallout between Carpenters and Neil Sedaka. The sublime vocal arrangement was composed by Richard Carpenter, and in his words, he says, "the song was difficult to sing, and Karen nailed it perfectly." Richard calls this one of Karen's greatest performances.

    Although "Solitaire" was not the huge hit as were "Please Mr. Postman" or "Only Yesterday," it still performed well on singles charts around the world and received a huge amount of airplay. The song's chart stats are as follows: #17 US, #12 Canada, #32 UK, #6 New Zealand, #61 Australia and #44 Japan.

    Neil Sedaka recorded and released "Solitaire" in 1972 on his album titled "Solitaire." Sedaka's recording of the song included members of the British band 10cc, who are known for the mid 70's hits "I'm Not in Love" and "The Things We Do for Love." Sedaka is also known for his stack of hits, such as "Breaking Up Is Hard to Do," Laughter in the Rain," "Oh, Carol" (written about Carole King), "Calendar Girl," "Happy Birthday Sweet Sixteen," "Next Door to an Angel." He has also written songs which were hits for others including "Stupid Cupid" for Connie Francis, "Love Will Keep Us Together" and "You Never Done It Like That" for Captain & Tennille. "Bad Blood" was a duet Sedaka did with Elton John which reached #1 on the charts.

- **Note from Rick Henry:** *In my mind this is absolutely one of Karen Carpenter's very best vocal interpretations. She takes this song all the way to the top. Karen sings this song with a flawless level of intensity that can only be matched by the best-of-the-best. Karen Carpenter just does not get any better. Richard's intense and intricate arrangement is as deserving of recognition as Karen's vocal performance. "Solitaire" rates amongst my ultimate, favorite Carpenters tracks.*

7. Happy (Tony Peluso / Diane Rubin / John Bettis) 3:51
    This song represents another technological triumph for Richard Carpenter. One of the main attractions of this power, pop tune is the ARP Odyssey Synthesizer solo, which brings the song to a close. It gives the song a lively, out-of-this-world feeling.

    Carpenters guitarist extraordinaire, Tony Peluso, wrote the melody and music for "Happy," so, of course, this song is based on driving guitar chords and rhythmic bass lines.

    Though not generally considered a "missed opportunity," some fans feel "Happy" would have been a strong single. The upbeat mood and the strong guitar work fit in well with what was topping the charts in 1975.

    "Happy" was released as the B-side on the single "Only Yesterday."

    - **Note from Rick Henry:** *This has been one of my all-time favorite songs since I first heard it in 1975; it easily ranks within my Top 10 favorite Carpenters tunes. I really wish Carpenters would have done more* *songs like this. I love every aspect of the song, most predominantly the synthesizer and Peluso's guitar work (I am a huge fan of the electric guitar). My favorite line in the song is when Karen sings, "If this is luck than let it ride. If it's the stars they're surely on my side."*

- **Side note on "Happy":** *I have searched high and low for information on songwriter Diane Rubin and come up with only one credit for her, that being this song. I figure she is either a pseudonym for another songwriter or maybe a friend-of-a-friend and has only worked on this one song.*

8. <u>(I'm Caught Between) Goodbye and I Love You (Richard Carpenter / John Bettis)</u> 4:06
Karen delivered this song with such a convincing soulfulness, that some speculate it may have been a reflection on her recent breakup with David Alley (a longtime associate of the Carpenters). The song, like 1976's "I Need to Be in Love," was autobiographical of the Carpenters' romantic dilemmas. When "Horizon" was released, lyricist John Bettis commented that "Goodbye and I Love You" was his and Richard's best collaboration.

The somewhat laid-back arrangement of this song packs a powerful punch. A smooth blend of acoustic and steel guitars adds an attractive, lazy feel that gives the song a slight, country music feel. The song tugs on the heartstrings of your emotions as it gently progresses. The feeling of heartbreak encapsulates the listener as Karen conveys the song's message backed by a gently, forlorn melody.

"(I'm Caught Between) Goodbye and I Love You" was used as the B-side of the single "There's a Kind of Hush (All Over the World)" which was released in February 1976.

> *So constantly stranded*
> *I can't understand it*
> *This double life you've handed me*
> *Is like the devil and the deep blue sea*

- **Note from Rick Henry:** *Simply put, I love this song. It's one of my favorites, but then again, everything from "Horizon" is one of my favorites.*

9. <u>Love Me for What I Am (Palma Pascale / John Bettis)</u>
3:30

"Love Me for What I Am" brings "Horizon" close to its sunset. The message is bold and self-explanatory by the song's title. Once again, Karen is so completely convincing that you, yourself, feel like you're living the lines of the song. This is one of the album's finest tunes with that trademark "chill factor." Karen's vocal is hauntingly bold and soulful. This song has a slightly stronger edge to it and reaches its pinnacle with a burning fuzz guitar solo by the legendary Tony Peluso. With this song Carpenters prove they are masters of the power ballad.

Songwriter Palma Pascale has said the idea for this song came to her in a dream. In an interview I did with her for the now defunct website The Carpenters Online, Palma commented, *"Love Me for What I Am" came in a most unusual way. I was asleep one night, and the words* ***"Love me for what I am, for simply being me. Don't love me for what you expect, or hope that I will be"*** *came in a dream. I remember arguing with myself about waking up to write them down. I didn't want to disturb myself, and write them down. I recall actually debating in my sleep the value of turning on the light, finding a pad and pen, etc., and would it be WORTH it! After all, I figured, you'll remember this tomorrow if it's that important, blah, blah, blah, anything to not have to get up! But the hand of destiny must have moved me to wake up, write it down, and go back to sleep."* The next day she finished the song within 45 minutes. After she recorded her demo of the song, she thought it would be perfect for the Carpenters to record. Palma brought home a list of entertainment manager's names and phone numbers. From that list Palma, of course, looked up Carpenters. She called the phone number and was referred to Ed Sulzer, who screened songs for

Carpenters. Two weeks later (dating November 1, 1973,) Palma received a letter from A&M Records stating that Richard Carpenter was interested in recording the song.

The original lyric to the song (as written by Palma) was different from what ended up being recorded by Carpenters. John Bettis was asked to rewrite some of the lyrics in order to better fit Karen's vocal tones and phrasing. To be sure, even though Bettis is listed in the songwriter credits, Palma Pascale wrote this song from beginning to end with a few lyric changes made by John Bettis. She gets full credit for the song (IMHO).

"Love Me for What I Am" is a favorite amongst Carpenters fans and is often mentioned on Carpenters forums, websites and Facebook pages. "Love Me for What I Am" ended up as the B-side of "Solitaire" and is rumored that it had been considered as an A-side single.

Carpenters recorded one more Palma Pascale tune titled "Box Office Movie King," which was intended for release on the 1976 album "A Kind of Hush." The song was never released and sits somewhere in the Carpenters "hidden treasures" vault of songs.

Carpenters superfan, Tim, had this to say about the song: *"Karen sings this Palma Pascale tune with beauty. It's well-suited for her voice, and it is a lovely song. Karen's reading of it is just right in this writer's opinion - longing in her voice - the loneliness shows through, and you can tell she's had more than her fair share of this kind of relationship, and she definitely needs someone to love her for being her, not the celebrity she now represents;. a beautiful read by Karen, well-produced by Rich, well-written by Palma."* (Tim was personal friends with Palma Pascale and has recorded music with her. You can read more about Tim and Palma at his blog "Martini's Musings").

- **Note from Rick Henry:** *I love this song for many reasons, but first I want to say a few words about*

Palma Pascale. Palma was one of the sweetest and most generous people I have ever known. When she set out to accomplish something she would put her complete heart and soul into it. She never did anything half-heartedly.

There is much about this song to love. I just love the lyrics, they're bold and strong. I really love the message: "You've got to love me for what I am, for simply being me." The song is a true anthem.

Then there's Richard's outstanding musical arrangement. It starts out understated and delicate and works its way to a full-fledged power ballad with the full range of instruments. Each instrument is strategically placed to complement each other and build a beautiful, musical masterpiece.

My favorite musical part of this song is Tony Peluso's smooth, fuzz guitar solo, which shows up about 3/4 of the way into the song. The guitar solo is intricate and polished and adds that extra bit of verve that turns the song into a dramatic masterpiece. The guitar also reminds us that Carpenters were very much in tune with what was new and cutting edge in popular music during the 1970's. Richard had a keen ear for keeping the music relevant and timeless, so much so that the majority of their music still sounds great to this very day. I feel Carpenters (with Tony Peluso) lead the way with power guitar chords in pop ballads resulting in, what is known today as, the power ballad.

Now, most important in this song is Karen's vocal performance. There is that tinge of sadness and melancholy in her voice. From the very first note, Karen sings this song to complete perfection. Her vocal timing is crisp and impeccably fresh. Her tones are clear and pure. She takes full advantage of her deep and dark lower voice, which is alarmingly beautiful and captivating. This is one of Karen's finest vocal performances of her entire career. Her voice is bold and powerful, yet sweet, delicate, full-bodied and *rich. It's vocal performances like this one which bring Karen a step above the rest and sets her in that league of all-time great vocalists.*

10. <u>Eventide (Richard Carpenter / John Bettis)</u> 1:33
After eight wonderfully crafted pop tunes that include a variety ranging from 40's big band, dark soulful ballads and propulsive, progressive power pop tunes, the album says goodnight with the second bookend piece "Eventide," which gently fades off into the horizon.

Written by Richard Carpenter and lyricist John Bettis, "Eventide" is the bookend companion to the dusky "Aurora." Both songs are identical in melody and length. Together they paint a beautifully haunting picture of the opening and closing of a day.

Thus, the day has ended, and we ride off into the sunset having grown from the wealth of emotions and joy given to us through song from this fantastic duo of Karen and Richard Carpenter.

<u>A Kind of Hush (click here to purchase)</u>
Released: June 11, 1976
Producer: Richard Carpenter
Associate Producer: Karen Carpenter
Arrangements & Orchestration: Richard Carpenter
All Vocals: Karen Carpenter & Richard Carpenter, MOR Chorale (I Need to Be in Love)
Keyboards: Richard Carpenter
Drums: Jim Gordon, Cubby O'Brien
Guitar: Tony Peluso
Bass: Joe Osborn
Tenor Sax: Bob Messenger
Baritone Sax: Jim Horn
Oboe and English Horn: Earl Dumler
Flute and Clarinet: Tom Scott
Flute: Bob Messenger (Sandy), David Shostac (I Need to Be in Love)
Tuba: Wes Jacobs

Vibes (Boat To Sail): Karen and Richard Carpenter
Harp: Gayle Levant
Cheek Pop (Goofus): Bob Messenger
Whistle (Can't Smile Without You): Doug Strawn
Engineer: Ray Gerhardt
Assistant Engineer: Dave Iveland
Mastering Engineer: Frank DeLuna
Art Direction: Roland Young
Photography: Ed Caraeff
Album Concept and Design: J. Scarkino & Co.
Special Thanks: Ed Sulzer, Ron Gorow and John Bettis
Chart Positions: US #33/ UK #3/ Japan #5/ Australia #57/ Canada #22/ New Zealand #15/ Norway #17/ Germany #42/ Netherlands #21
Certifications: Gold (US), Gold (UK)
Singles: There's a Kind of Hush/(I'm Caught Between) Goodbye and I Love You, I Need to Be in Love/Sandy, Goofus/Boat to Sail
Rick Henry's Rating: 8.4

It's June 11, 1976, and Carpenters' seventh studio album, "A Kind of Hush," has just been released. The album cover features a shot of Karen and Richard staring out into the world through a frosted window pane which gives a somewhat artsy, down-home feel. The backside of the cover shows the famous Carpenters logo, backwards, with the planet earth upon the red night sky, which lends itself to the title song "There's a Kind of Hush (All Over the World)." The inside lining of the album jacket is an autumn, orange-brown color with several rows of the Carpenters logo. Once you pull the record out it's housed in a good-quality inner sleeve with lyrics, with a somewhat pensive pose of Karen and Richard. The label on the record has the same picture as the backside of the album cover. It's obvious that A&M Records put a good amount of money into producing and packaging this record.

In the US, the album went on to be certified Gold and reached # 33. At this point in time, Carpenters were slowly losing their stride with the American public. On the worldwide scale, Carpenters were also beginning to lose some of their popularity, the album only charted in the Top 10 in two countries, # 3 in England and # 5 in Japan. Their previous album "Horizon" charted in the Top 10 in five countries and "Now & Then" in six countries.

"A Kind of Hush" was Carpenters' first album (not including "Ticket to Ride/Offering") to not have any Top 10 hits from it. The album was met with mixed reviews from Carpenters fans, notating the duo was showing signs of fatigue. Richard Carpenter himself said the album was inferior to their previous work, "Horizon."

Despite receiving mixed reviews from fans, it was the die-hard fans that fueled this album, maintaining their loyalty to Carpenters and praising songs such as "I Need to Be in Love," "One More Time," "You," "I Have You" and "Sandy."

1. <u>There's a Kind of Hush (All over the World)(Les Reed / Geoff Stephens)</u> 2:57
    Released three months before the album, "There's a Kind of Hush (All over the World)," this song was similar to "Please Mr. Postman" in that it was an upbeat remake of a 60's hit and was the first single from an upcoming album release. Unlike "Postman," "Hush" did not have the same punch or energy. It was, however, a refreshingly, pleasant surprise for fans and received heavy airplay throughout the US and many countries around the world. However, "There's a Kind of Hush" marked another significant drop in Carpenters popularity, being their first lead single (since "Ticket to Ride") not to reach the US Top Five and was their last Top 20 hit. The song reached #12 US, #11 Canada, #5 New Zealand, #22 UK, #27 Japan and #33 Australia.

    In 1967, Herman's Hermits took the song into the Top 10 in a dozen countries around the world including #4 US and #7 UK. The New Vaudeville Band, who is best remembered for their #1 hit "Winchester Cathedral," introduced a 1920's sounding rendition of "There's a Kind of Hush" in 1966. One of the song's co-writers, Geoff Stephens, was the leader and founder of the New Vaudeville Band.

Richard Carpenter has commented that even though the song was a hit, he wishes they never recorded the song.

2. You (Randy Edelman) 3:52
This is the third (and last) Randy Edelman composition recorded by Carpenters. The other two are "Piano Picker" and "I Can't Make Music" (you can read more on Edelman in the descriptions of these songs). Edelman reached #11 in 1976 with his remake of the Unit 4+2 hit "Concrete and Clay." He also made it onto the US singles chart in 1975 with "Everybody Wants to Find a Bluebird" reaching #92. Edelman himself released "You" as a single in 1977 and reached #49 with the song in the UK. In 1976, Randy Edelman married pop mega-star Jackie DeShannon (who also wrote the song "Boat to Sail"). "You" was originally recorded and featured on Edelman's 1976 album "Farewell Fairbanks" which also includes "Weekend in New England" (later a hit for Barry Manilow).

Having been associated with Edelman for over four years, Carpenters were more than eager to record another one of his compositions. Their recording of "I Can't Make Music," had become a favorite album track from "Now & Then," and "Piano Picker" was being used in concert to introduce Karen's fabulous drum solo. "You" is an inspirational track, which some people have commented has a spiritual emphasis in its lyric. Edelman, however, did not write the song as a religious song, but, instead, as a love song. "You" is an album highlight, and several Carpenters fans felt it would have been a good single. The song ended up receiving a marginal amount of radio airplay after the release of "A Kind of Hush." Due to its popularity, sheet music for the song was issued to music stores featuring a nice photo of Karen and Richard from their 1976 photo shoot. This sheet music is now long out-of-print and is a rare and hard-to-find item.

3. Sandy (Richard Carpenter / John Bettis) 3:42
Wind instruments drive this wistfully dramatic tune. It features a combo of flutes played by Bob Messenger and

renowned pop-jazz session man Tom Scott. Tom Scott also plays the clarinet on the song. The lyric was based on Richard Carpenter's girlfriend at the time, Sandy Holland, who was also Karen's hairdresser and assistant. Karen was never happy about the fact that Richard was dating Sandy. She felt it was a conflict of interest. Eventually Sandy was let go.

"Sandy" was released as the B-side to "I Need to Be in Love." Richard Carpenter featured an instrumental recording of this song on his "Pianist Arranger Composer Conductor" album, and you can hear the gorgeous background vocals of the Carpenters, of which Karen received credit on that album in 1998.

- **Note From Rick Henry:** *I find this to be a very pleasant song. I still listen to it on occasion and consider it to be one of the best from "A Kind of Hush." I especially enjoy Bob Messenger's flute at the end of the song.*

4. <u>Goofus (William Harold / Gus Kahn / Wayne King)</u> 3:09
When "A Kind of Hush" was released, "Goofus" received quite a bit of positive response from fans and also a fair amount of radio airplay. Due to fan and public demand, "Goofus" was released as a single on August 11, 1976, and reached US #56 (#82 Canada). Before the Carpenters recorded the song, it was already well known, having reached the Top 20 four times by four different artists in 1932 as an instrumental. In 1957, Wayne King wrote the lyrics, and the song was a hit again for country singer Phil Harris. Les Paul released his version in 1950 and reached #21 on the US charts (both Karen and Richard were fans of Les Paul). "Goofus" is also known as a popular clown theme played in circuses and carnivals throughout the US.

Gus Kahn is also known for writing the lyrics for the hits "Toot, Toot, Tootsie! (Goodbye)," "Carolina in the Morning," "It Had to Be You," "Yes Sir, That's My Baby," "Dream a Little Dream of Me" and several others.

Wes Jacobs joined Carpenters on "Goofus" with his low-pitched, vibrating tuba. This was the first time in ten years Jacobs had reunited with Carpenters. His tuba fit perfectly with the oddball nature of "Goofus." Toward the end of the song, Bob Messenger adds his own little personality to the song with his playful cheek pop.

- **Note from Rick Henry:** *Despite what some fans say about this song, it is one of my favorites. I love the upbeat, happy feel to it. The layering of vocals is excellent, and Richard Carpenter's musical arrangement is one of his most intricate. Each instrument is strategically placed to create a unique sound. It's the 1930's meets the 1970's... pure genius.*

5. <u>Can't Smile Without You (Chris Arnold / David Martin / Geoff Morrow)</u> 3:28
Many people (including some Carpenters fans) say this is a nice remake of the Barry Manilow song. The reality of the song is that Carpenters are the original artists to record the song, while it is Barry Manilow who did the remake. Back in the 70's, Carpenters were given the first opportunity to record new songs written by songwriters from many of the best-known publishing companies. They had first opportunity at these songs because they were considered guaranteed hit makers.

Carpenters never released "Can't Smile Without You" as an A-side single, although some fans feel the song would have been a better single than "Goofus." Manilow's version, which was recorded and released in 1978, was a huge hit reaching US #3.

Songwriter Geoff Morrow has also written several songs for Elvis Presley including "A Little Bit of Green," "This is the Story," "Let's Be Friends," and "Sweet Angeline." Songwriter David Martin says that one night in 1975 his wife gave him a greeting card, which across the top read "Can't Smile Without You." This gave him the idea for the song, and within a 30-minute drive home he had written the entire song.

In 1977, "Can't Smile Without You" was released as the B-side to the Top 40 hit "Calling Occupants of Interplanetary Craft." For this issue, Carpenters rerecorded the song with a new vocal, slightly revised lyrics and some added orchestration. This version of the song was included on the UK and European released compilation "Singles 1974-1978."

Doug Strawn, who plays saxophones, wind instruments and occasional keyboards provide the whistling part in this song.

- **Note from Rick Henry:** *Karen's voice shines like a bright sunny day on this song, which I always felt would have been a great as a single.*

6.   I Need to Be in Love (Richard Carpenter / John Bettis / Albert Hammond) 3:47

Most Carpenters fans consider this to be the album's strongest entry. The song originated as a snippet on a little orange, rehearsal cassette belonging to veteran singer/songwriter Albert Hammond ("It Never Rains in California"). John Bettis took the snippet and wrote an entire lyric (a sort of rough draft). He took the lyric and idea to Richard Carpenter, who then rewrote a good portion of the lyric and fine-tuned the song. Bettis has stated this is Carpenters' most autobiographical song and his favorite lyric he ever wrote for Karen. He also commented that this lyric came straight out of his heart for Karen. He really felt this one was especially for her.

The song features one of Karen's most soulful and yearning vocals and was her favorite Carpenters recording at the time.

"I Need to Be in Love" was released as a single on May 21, 1976, and reached #14 Ireland, #24 Canada, #25 US, #36 UK, #47 Australia, #62 Japan. In 1995 the song was rereleased as a single in Japan due to its popularity from being featured in a well-known Japanese drama, Miseinen. The song recharted and reached #5 in Japan.

As a songwriter, Albert Hammond has had a hugely, successful career having written or co-written hits such as "The Air That I Breathe" (#1 hit for The Hollies in 1974), "When I Need You" which went to #1 for Leo Sayer in 1977, "Easy to Love" a Top 40 hit for Leo Sayer, the classic "To All the Girls I've Loved Before" which was a #1 hit for Willie Nelson and Julio Iglesias in 1984. "Nothing's Gonna Stop Us Now" reached #1 in 1987 for Starship. Elton John and Aretha Franklin took "Through the Storm" into the Top 40 in 1989. Hammond's songs have been recorded by The Troggs, The Grassroots, Slim Whitman, Cilla Black, James Last, Art Garfunkel, Janis Ian, Diana Ross and many others.

7. One More Time (Lewis Anderson) 3:32
    This song is held in high regard by fans of Carpenters. Definitely a fan favorite. Richard Carpenter's arrangement is simple, uncluttered and dramatic, bringing Karen's voice to the front and center. Her vocal reading is brilliant as she conveys the emotions of despair and loneliness, yet retaining a feeling of warmth and familiarity.

    What makes this song especially appealing is the fact that the song does not contain any of the trademark Carpenters overdubbed or multi-layered vocals. It's just Karen Carpenter's singular voice. The result is astonishing. Karen was able to sing a delicate song and put her own sort of boldness into it.

    Lewis Anderson is a successful songwriter whose career spans several decades and genres. Most of his songs, though, have been recorded by country music artists such as Steve Wariner, Toby Keith, T.G. Sheppard, Alabama, Conway Twitty and others. Lewis Anderson's most successful single is B.J. Thomas' 1983 recording of "Whatever Happened to Old Fashioned Love" which reached #1 on the US and Canadian Country Music charts. It also made it to #93 on the US pop chart.

- **Note from Rick Henry:** *This is quite possibly my favorite song from "A Kind Of Hush." For the longest time, I have said that "Boat To Sail" is my favorite from the album, but upon reassessment I have to say in the long run the favorite has to be "One More Time." The song is majestic in a stripped-down sort of way.*

8. Boat to Sail (Jackie De Shannon) 3:31
"Boat to Sail" is the epitome of the laid-back, easygoing Southern California sound. You can almost feel the gentle waves of the ocean as you listen to this song.

Easily one of Richard's most outstanding and creative musical arrangements, the song includes layers of sound including electric vibes that give the song a sound of echoing chimes. Tony Peluso's guitar also adds to the overall ambiance of the song. The song's most prominent feature is the multi-layered reverb effect on the vocals giving the song an ethereal, dreamlike sound while putting a focus on the celestial "Beach Boys" type harmonies.

Electric vibes are played on an electronic vibraphone, which is this keyboard-looking type of instrument that is struck with a mallet(s) much like drums, and is considered part of the percussion family.

Jackie DeShannon is best known for her hits "What the World Needs Now is Love" (written by Hal David & Burt Bacharach) and "Put a Little Love in Your Heart," a song which she co-wrote with Jimmy Holiday and Randy Myers. DeShannon is also the co-writer of Kim Carnes' 1981 super-hit "Bette Davis Eyes." Toward the end of the song as it fades away, Karen sings, "DeShannon is back" which mirrors another A&M act, the Captain and Tennille, with their chart-topper "Love Will Keep Us Together" where they end with, "Sedaka is back."

Brian Wilson, who is mentioned in the song's lyric, sang background vocals on De Shannon's version, which appeared on her 1975 album "New Arrangement." De

Shannon married songwriter and film composer Randy Edleman in 1976 (right around the time "A Kind of Hush" was released). "A Kind of Hush" also includes "You," a tune written by Edelman. "You" and "Boat To Sail" are husband and wife counterparts.

- **Note from Rick Henry:** *This is one of my all-time favorite Carpenters songs. It's a slight bit unusual for them and would have fit well on the album "Passage." Tony Peluso's guitar work is very effective in conveying the song's easygoing mood. The use of electric vibes (performed by Karen and Richard) give the song a shimmering, chiming sound throughout. The layered vocals bring about a very attractive, sunny-day effect. I love the lyrics in this song - makes you feel like you're on the beach.*
  I consider this to be one of the Carpenters' most creative songs in their entire repertoire. It is my favorite from "A Kind of Hush" (I know I just said "One More Time" is ultimately my favorite on the album... I guess I'm torn between two favorites).

9. <u>I Have You (Richard Carpenter / John Bettis)</u> 3:37
   This charming song features an excellent, double-tracking of Karen's voice on the chorus, which makes the chorus pop out and gives it an unusual, yet alluring sound. Karen harmonizes with her lead vocal showcasing the depth and emotion in her voice.

   The reserved musical arrangement gives the song an intimacy that really works well with Karen's haunting vocal.

   "I Have You" was released as an A-side single in 1978 with "Sweet, Sweet Smile" on the B-side. In Japan, "I Have You" was used as the B-side to "Breaking Up is Hard to Do." The song was also the B-side on the international releases of "All You Get from Love is a Love Song" and "Sweet, Sweet Smile."

10. <u>Breaking Up Is Hard to Do (Neil Sedaka / Howard Greenfield)</u> 2:35 -

Neil Sedaka was the opening act for Carpenters during their 1975 tour. In that same year, Carpenters terminated Sedaka's contract due to personal and/or artistic reasons. In turn, Carpenters received a small amount of negative publicity. The rumor was they fired Neil Sedaka because he was upstaging Carpenters. In 1976, Carpenters recorded "Breaking Up Is Hard to Do" as a possible way of bridging the gap. The title of the song is ironic considering the situation between Carpenters and Sedaka.

While listening to the song you can hear Karen and Richard and their band in the background laughing and talking and someone saying, "Hey, Karen!" The song leaves you with the impression that Karen, Richard and the band were having a great time recording this upbeat, yet simple song. Although the song is not Carpenters at their best, it is an enjoyable track.

"Breaking Up Is Hard to Do" backed with "I Have You" was released as a single and reached #71 in Japan.

Interestingly, Richard Carpenter wrote the strings arrangement for Neil Sedaka's 1975 ballad re-recording of "Breaking Up Is Hard to Do." Some fans have speculated on the possibility of a ballad recording of the song hiding in the Carpenters vaults of the unreleased.

Passage (click here to purchase)
Released: September 23, 1977
Producer: Richard Carpenter
Associate Producer: Karen Carpenter
Arrangements & Orchestration: Richard Carpenter
Orchestration: Peter Knight (I Just Fall in Love Again, On the Balcony of the Casa Rosada/Don't Cry for Me Argentina and Calling Occupants of Interplanetary Craft)
Vocal Arrangements: Gene Perling (B'wana She No Home)
All Vocals: Karen Carpenter & Richard Carpenter
Acoustic and Electric Piano: Richard Carpenter
Piano: Pete Jolly (B'wana She No Home)

Tack Piano: Tom Hensley (Sweet, Sweet Smile, Man Smart, Woman Smarter), Richard Carpenter (Man Smart, Woman Smarter)

Electric Piano: Larry Muhoberac (B'wana She No Home)

Drums: Ron Tutt, Ed Green

Steel Drums: Vince Charles

Percussion: Wally Snow, Tommy Vig

Conga: Jerry Steinholtz (B'wana She No Home), King Erickson (Man Smart, Woman Smarter)

Electric Guitar: Tony Peluso, Ray Parker (All You Get from Love Is a Love Song)

Acoustic Guitar: Tony Peluso (Sweet, Sweet Smile), Lee Ritenour (Two Sides), Jay Graydon (Two Sides)

Steel Guitar: Jay Dee Maness

Bass: Joe Osborn

Fiddle: Bobby Bruce (Sweet, Sweet Smile)

Banjo: Larry McNealy (Sweet, Sweet Smile)

Tenor Sax: Tom Scott (B'wana She No Home, All You Get from Love Is a Love Song), Jackie Kelso (Man Smart, Woman Smarter)

Baritone Sax: David Luell (Man Smart, Woman Smarter), Kurt McGettrick (Man Smart, Woman Smarter)

Oboe: Earl Dumler

Alto Flute: Tom Scott

Harp: Gayle Levant

Background Singers: Julia Waters Tillman, Maxine Willard Waters and Carlena Williams (All You Get from Love Is a Love Song)

Orchestra: Overbudget Philharmonic (I Just Fall in Love Again, On the Balcony of the Casa Rosada/Don't Cry for Me Argentina and Calling Occupants of Interplanetary Craft)

Orchestra Conductor: Peter Knight (I Just Fall in Love Again, On the Balcony of the Casa Rosada/Don't Cry for Me Argentina and Calling Occupants of Interplanetary Craft)

Choral Singers: Gregg Smith Singers (I Just Fall in Love Again, On the Balcony of the Casa Rosada/Don't Cry for Me Argentina and Calling Occupants of Interplanetary Craft)

Announcer: Dennis Heath (On the Balcony of the Casa Rosada)

Peron: William Feuerstein (On the Balcony of the Casa Rosada)

Che: Jonathan Marks (On the Balcony of the Casa Rosada)

Synthesizer: Richard Carpenter (Calling Occupants of Interplanetary Craft)

DJ: Tony Peluso (Calling Occupants of Interplanetary Craft)
Engineer: Ray Gerhardt, Roger Young and Dave Iveland
Mastering Engineer: Bernie Grundman
Art Direction: Roland Young
Cover Art: Lou Beach
Album Concept and Design: Junie Osaki
Liner Notes: Tom Nolan
Special Thanks: Ed Sulzer, Ron Gorow and John Bettis
Personal Management: Jerry Weintraub, Management Three
Chart Positions: Japan #7, UK #12, Australia #48, US #49, Canada #57
Certifications: Gold (UK)
Singles: All You Get from Love Is a Love Song/I Have You; Calling Occupants of Interplanetary Craft/Can't Smile Without You; Sweet, Sweet Smile/I Have You; Don't Cry for Me Argentina/Calling Occupants of Interplanetary Craft
Rick Henry's Rating: 9.3

After a year and a half of sagging sales and no Top 10 hits from their previous album, "A Kind of Hush," a change in musical direction came to play. This was the first (and only) Carpenters album not to feature a Richard Carpenter / John Bettis composition. Richard Carpenter looked upon other songwriters for inspiration and the change of direction that was much needed. Richard gathered a potpourri of songs that showcased the diverse talents of Carpenters. He attained these songs from songwriter/musicians as varied as Michael Franks (smooth jazz), Klaatu (Canadian Beatlesque), Juice Newton (country) and Andrew Lloyd Weber.

Released on September 23, 1977, critics and radio programmers were saying that "Passage" would bring Carpenters back into the Top 10. The album received favorable reviews by critics, but after all the hoopla the album peaked just outside the Top 40 in the US reaching #49. In other countries the album sold well; it was a solid Top 15 hit in England and Japan.

Not only was the sound different, but also the look was different. The album packaging was the first not to include a picture of Karen and Richard anywhere on or inside the album. The colorfully, artistic album cover suggests the music inside contains a flair and liveliness that was absent from the previous Carpenters album. They even redesigned the famous Carpenters logo. This was the first and only Carpenters album not to contain the classic Carpenters logo. This upset some Carpenters fans. Even though the majority of Carpenters fans like "Passage," there are some who call the album a sellout and do not like it. Overall the album is respected for its diversity in both music style and musicianship.

1. <u>B'wana She No Home (Michael Franks)</u> 5:36
"B'wana She No Home" marked a major shift in perspective concerning the future of Carpenters. The song opened the album, and immediately you knew this was not going to be your typical Carpenters record. We got a hint of this change in direction just from the album cover alone, but hearing the first percussive thud followed by a spirited keyboard and finally joined by electrifying guitar chords the hunch is confirmed. Carpenters have dabbled with jazz-fusion in the past with "All I Can Do" (1969) and "Another Song (1970), but never to this degree of intricacy or authenticity. This song would have fit well being played alongside anything from Grover Washington, Jr.'s "Mister Magic" (1975) album.

"B'wana She No Home" was recorded live in the studio - all the musicians, vocalists, technicians, engineers, producers and others were there to record the song. In most Carpenters recordings, different parts would be recorded at different times. One day, the bass and drums will be recorded, while in another session, the keyboards and vocals will be done and so forth. Being recorded live in the studio gave "B'wana She No Home" a jam-band sound as well as giving all the musicians the opportunity to play off of each other. Pete Jolly and Tom Scott give us a fantastic piano and sax duo in this format.

This is the first Carpenters song in which someone other than Richard Carpenter composed the vocal arrangement for Karen. Gene Puerling (aka Gene Perling) scored the vocal arrangement for "B'wana She

No Home." Puerling created and led the jazz vocal groups The Hi-Lo's and The Singer's Unlimited. Randy Schmidt, the author of the book "Little Girl Blue," stated that Puerling's previous work with vocal jazz ensembles makes him the perfect fit for Karen's voice. In 1982, Puerling won a Grammy Award for his vocal arrangement of "A Nightingale Sang in Berkeley Square" as recorded by the Manhattan Transfer. He's also worked with vocalists such as Frank Sinatra and Rosemary Clooney. With "B'wana She No Home," Puerling was able to reach back to his experience in arranging Latin jazz vocals in his work with the Singer's Unlimited. Puerling was able to bring out a more playful, yet authoritative side of Karen's voice, which sits well with the song's chunkier sound.

In 1978 "B'wana She No Home" was chosen to be the B-side of the single "I Believe You." This song is one of a handful of Carpenters songs that has not yet been featured on any Carpenters compilations.

Written by mellow, jazz artist Michael Franks (Franks had hits with "Popsicle Toes" 1975, "The Lady Wants to Know" 1977 and "Your Secret's Safe with Me" 1985). Franks' version of "Bwana She No Home" resides on his 1977 album "Sleeping Gypsy," which also includes the hits "The Lady Wants to Know." Franks' "Sleeping Gypsy" employs a slight, Brazilian feel in its style and lyrics. The song "Antonio's Song," is a tribute to Brazilian trendsetter Antonio Carlos Jobim, best known for his composition "The Girl from Ipanema." "B'wana She No Home" displays Franks' skill in turning out witty lyrics and telling a story. Michael Franks based this song loosely on a time when he was out of town and musician friend Dan Hicks was staying at his house.

- **Note from Rick Henry:** *This is my favorite song from the album. That's saying a lot because this album contains at least three other songs which I consider to be all-time favorites of mine. I like the beefiness of the song and Tony Peluso's guitar work. Quite a few Carpenters fans have expressed their confusion with* *the meaning of this song. My take has always been that the focal person (in this case Karen Carpenter) is a wealthy recluse. She has a servant from Guayaquil, Ecuador, who most likely is illegal. She has ordered her servant to tell anybody who comes to the door to say she is not home. The term B'wana is a term of respect much like the terms "sir" or "ma'am." Though B'wana is strict in her orders in making sure her servant does everything right, even down to speaking proper English, she is also generous with her servant, letting her drive her car and spend her money.*

2. <u>All You Get from Love Is a Love Song (Steve Eaton)</u> 3:47
This was the first peek people had of the upcoming album. "All You Get from Love Is a Love Song" was released five months prior to "Passage." Fans were delighted with the new, high-steppin' sound that was designed to take Carpenters back into the Top 10. Despite the enthusiasm behind this single, it did not bring Carpenters back into the Top 10, but it did open the door to a fresh new direction to usher the Carpenters into the late 70's.

Songwriter Steve Eaton wrote the song in late 1970 / early 1971. It was about a girlfriend who ended a relationship with him. He was downtrodden and decided to climb up Scott Mountain (Pocatello, Idaho) so he could be alone. It was up in Scott Mountain that he came up with the idea for "All You Get from Love Is a Love Song." Other Steve Eaton songs include: "Out on the Road" recorded by Anne Murray, "Rag Doll" by Art Garfunkel and "I'll Still Be Loving You" recorded by Lee Greenwood.

Before Carpenters recorded the song, the Righteous Brothers on their 1974 album "The Sons of Mrs. Righteous" released it. Tom Scott masterfully provides the tenor sax solo, which really keeps the sizzle going in this song. Ray Parker, Jr. ("Ghostbusters," "You Can't Change That") joins Tony Peluso on electric guitar. When it's all put together "All You Get from Love Is a

Love Song" is a flavorful, upbeat, toe-tapping, samba-like tune.

Released on May 2, 1977, this was the first single released from "Passage." The song just made the Top 40 reaching US 35. In other parts of the world, the song reached #38 Canada, #68 Japan and #89 Australia.

- **Note from Rick Henry:** *I loved this song right from the first time I heard it. It came as a surprise. I found out about the song when I was visiting my favorite music store, and I saw the single in the new release bin. Of course, my heart skipped a beat when I saw it, and I instantly bought it. I remember thinking the song was a fresh and colorful sound. It had a little spice about it.*

3. <u>I Just Fall in Love Again (Stephen Dorff / Larry Herbstritt / Harry Lloyd / Gloria Sklerov)</u> 4:05 - This classic, power ballad is one which many Carpenters fans claim should have been released as a single. Richard Carpenter had considered releasing it, but didn't due to the length of the song. He felt it was too long for radio airplay and did not see any conceivable way of properly editing it.

The legendary Peter Knight orchestrated the song and took it over the top with its dreamy interpretation. Peter Knight is well-remembered for his work with The Moody Blues on their colossal album, "Days of the Future Passed." "I Just Fall in Love Again" is complete with a soaring, guitar solo by Tony Peluso and trademark Carpenters oboe and keyboard sounds. Karen Carpenter delivers this song with a compelling richness and maturity, capitalizing on the understated soulfulness of her full-bodied voice. Both Anne Murray and Dusty Springfield have recorded this song, though not quite with the same energy and intensity as Karen.

Songwriter Larry Herbstritt says the initial idea for the song came after he had read a book on Beethoven and then listened to some of the classical genius's compositions. After composing the chorus of "I Just Fall in Love Again," he took it to composer friend Stephen Dorff for his opinion. Dorff assessed the chorus as a verse much in need of a chorus. Herbstritt took his chorus back to the drawing board and added to it. He then took the song back to Steve Dorff who liked what he heard this time and added his touch to the melody and wrote some of the initial lyrics. Dorff and Herbstritt took the song to Snuff Garrett's company and employed Gloria Sklerov and Harry Lloyd to write the lyrics.

"I Just Fall in Love Again" suffers the same identity crisis as "Can't Smile Without You." Carpenters originally recorded both songs first. Since each song was a hit for another artist, it is these artists the public thinks are the originals (Barry Manilow with "Can't Smile Without You" and Anne Murray with "I Just Fall in Love Again"). Carpenters recorded "I Just Fall in Love Again" in 1977 while Anne Murray recorded it in 1979.

4. On the Balcony of the Casa Rosada/Don't Cry for Me Argentina (Andrew Lloyd Webber / Tim Rice) 8:13
    "Don't Cry for Me Argentina" is a huge fan favorite. Many fans claim this as one of Karen's best vocal performances. On the flipside some of the same fans also claim to be annoyed with (or not interested in) "On the Balcony of the Casa Rosada." But as it goes, this opener, in part, is what makes the Carpenters' recording of "Don't Cry for Me Argentina" the definitive recording (definitive of recordings done by pop artists). "On the Balcony of the Casa Rosada" depicts a scene from the balcony of the Casa Rosada (which is to Argentina as the White House is to the US) in which Juan Peron (the newly elected president) is introduced to the citizens of Argentina. From the masses of people, Che (a diplomat and revolutionary) speaks out about his excitement. William Feuerstein (Juan Peron) and Jonathan Marks (Che) were employed to perform the parts on "Passage." Dennis Heath performs the part of the announcer. Heath's friendship with Karen and Richard extends back to the mid-60's when Richard was attending Cal State Long Beach. By including this prelude the recording

now turns into more than just a mere song but a musical event.

If that's not enough, the song was more than just a musical event - it also became a news media event. It was hailed as the largest recording session ever in the history of popular music, with over 160 people present to record the song. This fact made it into the entertainment section of newspapers across the US and on the nightly news on the three major networks.

Despite the fact that "On the Balcony of the Casa Rosada" turns this into a musical event, it is still Karen's vocal interpretation that makes the song the classic it is. Karen Carpenter was born to sing this song. Both Julie Covington and Patti Lupone have done spectacular renditions of the song, but it is Karen who seems to capture the song's emotion. It's as if Karen Carpenter was peeking into Eva Peron's soul as she sang these words. Karen sang the song with boldness and strength. She sang as if she had not a fear in the world. Karen sang this song to perfection.

5. <u>Sweet, Sweet Smile (Juice Newton / Otha Young)</u> 3:02
The song opens with a funky, rhythmic, electric guitar played by Tony Peluso which, with in seconds, is joined by the band which includes Tom Hensley on tack piano, Larry McNealy on banjo (the banjo adds a great C&W sound), Bobby Bruce on fiddle, Ron Tutt (from Elvis Presley's band) on drums and Joe Osborn on bass guitar. The arrangement is full, up-tempo and lively, like we've never heard Carpenters before.

It was Karen Carpenter who initially heard this song (on a pre-release of a then upcoming Juice Newton album). Karen felt the song was right for Carpenters, and they ended up recording it. "Sweet, Sweet Smile" was the third single release from "Passage." The song received a fair amount of radio airplay in early 1978, and several expected it to reach the Top 10. And, it did reach the Top 10, but on the country music charts where it peaked at #8. On the pop chart, the song reached #19

Belgium, #22 Germany, #33 Canada, #40 UK, #44 US, #59 Japan and #100 Australia. Since 1978 "Sweet, Sweet, Smile" has remained a popular favorite, being used in country and western clubs for line dances throughout the US and other parts of the world.

Juice Newton wrote the upbeat "Sweet, Sweet Smile" with her husband Otha Young. Newton later went on to have her own string of hits, including "Angel of the Morning," "Queen of Hearts," "The Sweetest Thing (I've Ever Known)," "Love's Been a Little Bit Hard on Me" and "Break It to Me Gently."

- **Note from Rick Henry:** *I love Juice Newton, I love Karen Carpenter and I love "Sweet, Sweet Smile!"*

6. <u>Two Sides (Scott E. Davis)</u> 3:28
"Two Sides" is a special song to the many Carpenters fans that are captured by the word play in the lyrics and Karen's convincing delivery. Some fans (and critics) have thought the song was strong enough for single release.

It's a guitar lover's treat! This mildly, country-flavored song showcases an array of very well placed and beautifully performed guitars. Included are two acoustic guitars, a magnificent pedal steel guitar and Tony Peluso's ever-captivating electric guitar. Jazz guitarist, Lee Ritenour, plays one of the acoustic guitars.

The lyrics are one of the song's most compelling attributes. "Two Sides" speaks of coming to terms with a relationship that just isn't working out and having the strength to say "Goodbye." The song is pieced together with patience and thought. It touches on all the different emotions one feels in such a situation.

Above all is Karen's, once again, triumphant vocal. She delivers the song with ease and a subtle, sort of soul. She conveys the message of the song in a relaxed, yet self-confident manner.

There's a slight mystery as to the identity of the songwriter. The credits list the songwriter as Scott E. Davis, which is an alias used by popular singer-songwriter Mac Davis. At this point it has not been confirmed that the songwriter of "Two Sides" is, indeed, Mac Davis. This could just be a coincidence. Mac Davis has done some work with Carpenters. In 1971, he was the opening for Carpenters during part of the US tour. He also appeared on an episode of Carpenters' 1971 summer series "Make Your Own Kind of Music."

- **Note from Rick Henry:** *There is so much I love about this song. I like the mood the song conveys: a somewhat melancholy touch that in a roundabout way is a song of courage in being able to walk away from a relationship that is not productive. I like the strength in the attitude of this song. I also like the fact that it has a mild country flavor to it. Carpenters did such an excellent job with those country-esque tunes ("Goodbye and I Love You," "Reason to Believe," "Those Good Old Dreams" and several others). I also like the quartet of guitars -- really gives the song that laid-back, Southern California sound. But my favorite part comes near the end of the song when Karen sings that last "goodbye" and holds the note until it fades into obscurity. Ahhhh... that right there is the "chill factor" in this song.*

7. Man Smart, Woman Smarter (Norman Span) 4:22
This song displays the tongue-in-cheek side of Carpenters, yet maintaining quality in musicianship. Quite a few Carpenters fans dislike this song, mainly due to the extended instrumental part at the end with the googling and gargling sound effects.

"Man Smart, Woman Smarter" is a calypso song, which has been around for more than 50 years and has an interesting history.
* Harry Belafonte first brought it to fame in 1956 when it was released on his #1 album "Calypso." Folk music legend, Alan Lomax, also recorded the song around the same time.

* In an episode aired March 15, 1957, the song was performed on television's "I Love Lucy" by a band comprising of Lucy, Ricky, Little Ricky, Ethel and Fred.
* In early 1977, Robert Palmer made his debut on the singles chart with the song.
* "Man Smart, Woman Smarter" was introduced to the Grateful Dead in 1981, and from then on the song became a regular part of the Grateful Dead's live show.
* In the late 90's reggae artists Chaka Demus and Pliers cover the song.

The Carpenters took the song and turned it into a rocker with hints of humor. The song has an impressive display of drums, including congas and steel drums. Again, we're treated to Tony Peluso's energetic electric guitar and Leon Russell (writer of "Superstar," "A Song For You" and "This Masquerade") bangs on the piano.

The song jolts along with an extended jam-style instrumental solo at the end with crazy sound effects switching back and forth between the left and right channels of the stereo speakers. This is quite an interesting, almost alternative music, effect. The Carpenters score again with diversity and a heart of experimentation.

Songwriter Norman Span is a calypso musician/songwriter. Throughout the 30's and 40's he wrote quite a few calypso numbers which have gone on to become classics. Norman Span also goes by the name of King Radio. King Radio started performing the song in the 1930's in Trinidad Carnival tents. In 1936, he recorded it for Decca Records. Norman Span also goes by the name of One-Eye Norman Span.

8. Calling Occupants of Interplanetary Craft (The Recognized Anthem of World Contact Day)(Terry Draper / John Woloschuk) 7:08
    In the liner notes of "Passage," the songwriting credits of the song are listed as, Words and Music by Klaatoons. Canadian group Klaatu wrote and recorded this song for their 1976 album, simply titled Klaatu. On that album,

the songwriting credits also listed Klaatoons. It wasn't until the 2000's that the identities of the songwriters were revealed as Terry Draper and John Woloschuk. Klaatu came to fame when rumors led to speculation that they were the Beatles performing under an assumed name. In an interview which has appeared in "The Carpenters Online Interviews" e-book, Klaatu member, Dee Long, has mentioned because of Carpenters, "Calling Occupants..." made a lot of money for Terry and John.

The Carpenters' recording was an enormous undertaking with 160 people involved. The famed Peter Knight orchestrated and arranged this galactic event. Klaatu relied heavily on electronic sound effects and synthesizers to create their illusion of outer space. Whereas, the Carpenters used a full orchestra with swirling violins, haunting pipe organ, Tony Peluso's out of this world guitar solos, Richard's spacey electronic piano and a fabulous marching band. Rounding it all out is Karen's fantastic voice. The vocalist of countless pop-ballads proves she's more than just your average singer as she aptly croons the galactic melody. The album version of the song opens with a confused radio DJ played by guitarist Tony Peluso. Peluso also played the DJ in the "Oldies Medley" on the "Now and Then" album.

"Calling Occupants..." was released as a single on September 9, 1977, and reached #1 Ireland, #9 UK and Canada, #13 Australia, #18 New Zealand and #32 US. The song also became a Top 10 hit in Southern California where it enjoyed airplay on FM album rock radio stations, which was unheard of for the Carpenters until then. "Calling Occupants..." received a Grammy Award nomination for Richard's galactic musical arrangement. In many ways, this song was a huge triumph for the Carpenters.

After the song had been released as a single, the Carpenters Fan Club received several letters asking when World Contact Day would be. Richard Carpenter had erroneously answered that there was no "World

Contact Day." According to John Woloschuk, "World Contact Day" does exist. It happened in March 1953, when the "International Flying Saucer Bureau" (IFSB) organized its first World Contact Day. The members of the IFSB gathered in April 1953 in an attempt to collectively send out a telepathic message to visitors from outer space. The message began with the phrase, "calling occupants of interplanetary craft."

From beginning to end, "Passage" succeeds at entertaining the listener in a way no other Carpenters album has ever done. "Passage" is the Carpenters' most diverse album musically, while maintaining the quality musicianship found on all previous Carpenters albums.

- **Note from Rick Henry:** *I have always liked "Calling Occupants" quite a bit. Yes, the song does tend to get longish but it's the creativity of it, the tempo changes, the movements, Karen's voice, the guitar work. It's a pop music masterpiece.*

Christmas Portrait (click here to purchase)
Released: October 13, 1978
Producer: Richard Carpenter
Associate Producer: Karen Carpenter
Arrangements & Orchestration: Nick Perito, Billy May, Peter Knight, Richard Carpenter
All Vocals: Karen Carpenter & Richard Carpenter, The Tom Bahler Chorale, OK Chorale
Keyboards: Richard Carpenter, Pete Jolly
Drums: Ron Tutt, Cubby O'Brien, Barry Morgan
Bass: Joe Osborn, Peter Morgan
Tenor Sax: Bob Messenger
Harp: Dorothy Remsen, Skaila Kanga
Engineer: Ray Gerhardt, Roger Young, Dave Iveland
Mastering Engineer: Arnie Acosta
Art Direction and Design: Tim Bryant
Photography: Ed Caraeff
Special Thanks: Ed Sulzer
Chart Positions: US #114/ UK #104
Certifications: Platinum (US), Gold (Canada)

Singles: Merry Christmas Darling, Santa Claus Is Coming to Town, Christmas Song, Ave Maria
Rick Henry's Rating: 9.8

Karen and Richard Carpenter had a lifelong fondness for Christmas music. With the idea of recording a Christmas album simmering for several years, "Christmas Portrait" was finally realized due to the Carpenters' preparation for their second television special, "The Carpenters at Christmas," which aired on December 9, 1977. Beginning in the summer of 1977, Karen and Richard decided, as they began selecting and recording the music for this television special, that the time was right to record, at long last, an album dedicated to Christmas music.

Richard commented, "By the time Karen and I began recording this album I was not interested in more than production work. So I turned over most of the arranging to veterans Peter Knight and Billy May." He goes on to say, "'Christmas Portrait' is really Karen's album, and should have been titled accordingly, not the Carpenters." This was mostly due to Richard's dealing with his sleeping pill problem at the time.

"Christmas Portrait" was 14 months in the making, and was released on October 13, 1978. At that point in time, this was their most expensive album to produce. The number of tracks recorded for this LP pushed the envelope for an album made during that time frame — it had a total of seventeen tracks, which was almost unheard of at the time, as an LP record seldom had room for that many tracks. Many songs cross-faded with each other, weaving an expansive medley and fine tapestry of textures, colors and moods of the season.

[As an interesting side note on why it took 14 months to make this album and to provide context, the Carpenters actually took several breaks from recording to work on other projects. They taped their third television special "Space Encounters," which aired on May 17, 1978. Karen and Richard also recorded several songs for an album, which was to be released in 1979. Some of the songs recorded were: "I Believe You," "Where Do I Go From Here?" the studio recording of "Thank You for the Music" and a full version of "Dancing in the Street." Unfortunately, the album was never completed, but since then, many of the tracks have been released on various compilations.]

"Christmas Portrait" features a varied selection of songs ranging from the sacred to traditional Christmas tunes to some lesser-known songs. Many of the tracks on "Christmas Portrait" are from the original Spike Jones Christmas album, which Karen and Richard have said is one of the best Christmas albums ever. The emotions on "Christmas Portrait" go from upbeat and cheerful to the thought-provoking, reflective and soul- stirring. The Carpenters did more than just sing these tunes — they woke them up and breathed new life into them. They restored seldom-heard verses to classic tunes and added extra sounds and textures to give the feeling of actually being in Toyland or experiencing that first snowfall.

For "Christmas Portrait," Richard and Karen retained the bulk of their regular, backup-band as well as employing the best musicians available. The arrangement for most of the album is reminiscent of the style of classic 1940's movie musicals. Peter Knight crafted the majority of the musical arrangements with great inspiration and care. Knight was previously known for his superb work on the Moody Blues' classic album "Days of the Future Passed." Knight has also worked on many other Carpenters songs, including the 1977 hit "Calling Occupants of Interplanetary Craft" and one of Karen's favorites, "Look to Your Dreams." Billy May also arranged many songs for "Christmas Portrait." May is a veteran who has worked with Frank Sinatra, and constructed the beautifully intense arrangement for Carpenters' "I Can Dream, Can't I?" Richard did the arrangements for "O Come, O Come Immanuel" and the classic "Merry Christmas Darling." Each musical arrangement is unique, detailed, crisp, clean and multi-dimensional. The songs are filled with a thrilling and chilling mix of instruments, including keyboards, guitars, bass, drums, harp, oboe, and Bob Messenger's tenor sax. Messenger has the ability to create an emotional excitement with his inspiring sax solos, as he has done so beautifully on the songs "A Song for You" and "Rainy Days and Mondays." Another wonderful example of Messenger's finesse is on "Have Yourself a Merry Little Christmas," which is a favorite from "Christmas Portrait."

Many critics agree that "Christmas Portrait" is one of the finest holiday albums of all-time. When asked how she felt about recording the Christmas album, Karen replied, "I enjoy doing this type of music all year round, which has been proved, because it took us 14 months to cut this album, and while people were walking down the aisles saying, 'Why in heaven's name are you doing Christmas stuff in the middle of August?' it never occurred to me, 'cause I could do it anytime of the day or night, anytime of the year." The Carpenters had such a good time recording "Christmas Portrait" that they recorded way too many songs for one album. The unused "extra" tracks and additional recordings by Richard were released in a later album, "An Old-Fashioned Christmas" in October 1984.

"Christmas Portrait" is Christmas music at its ultimate best, and has become a perennial holiday favorite.

The album originally peaked at #150 on the US album chart in 1978 and has made it onto the album charts several times since then. In December 2011, the album re-entered the US album chart at #150 and eventually achieved a new chart peak position of #126. But wait - it doesn't end here - in 2012, the album returned to the charts, and in December 2012, it reached an even higher peak position at #114... needless to say, fans were ecstatic. There is going to be a big promotion to push "Christmas Portrait" into the Top 100 in 2013.

OVERTURE
The overture consists of "Deck the Halls," "I Saw Three Ships," "Have Yourself a Merry Little Christmas," "God Rest Ye Merry Gentlemen," "Away in a Manger," "What Child is This," "Carol of the Bells," and "O Come All Ye Faithful (Adeste Fideles)." The music to "Deck the Halls" is believed to be Welsh in origin from a tune called "Nos Galan" from the 16th Century, and the unknown author of the lyrics is thought to be American. The author and composer for "I Saw Three Ships" are unknown, but the song is believed to be an English carol from the Victorian era. "Have Yourself a Merry Little Christmas" is discussed a little bit later here and in the section on Karen's vocal rendition of it. Reputedly dating back to the 15th Century, the lyrics of "God Rest Ye Merry

Gentlemen" are traditional Olde English and were sung to the gentry by town watchmen who earned additional money during the Christmas season in this manner. With the words by an unknown author and originally published in 1885, "Away in a Manger" was composed by William J. Kirkpatrick in 1895. The words to "What Child is This?" were written by William Chatterton Dix in 1865, with the music borrowed from the 16th Century English melody of love lost, "Greensleeves." "Carol of the Bells" is discussed later in the section on Richard's full rendition of it. The text of "O Come All Ye Faithful" was originally written in Latin (Adeste Fideles), with the music composed by John Reading in the early 1700's, and the text attributed to John Wade and, later, Frederick Oakley in 1841 for the more familiar English translation.

Peter Knight's arrangements and orchestrations vary in mood and style within this instrumental medley and include a few surprises, notably giving a "Big Band" treatment to "God Rest Ye Merry Gentlemen" and sprinkling bits of the refrain of "Jingle Bells" into "Have Yourself a Merry Little Christmas."

CHRISTMAS WALTZ
First published in 1954, "Christmas Waltz" was written by lyricist Sammy Cahn and composer Jule Styne, who have contributed to many Broadway musicals and movies. It had been recorded through the years by crooners such as Frank Sinatra, Robert Goulet, Andy Williams and Harry Connick, Jr.

Arranged and orchestrated by Peter Knight, "Christmas Waltz" is the first song that features Karen's crystal-clear voice on the album, piercing through the sweep of instrumental numbers in the overture with a dramatic entrance, vivid imagery and warm wishes for the holiday season.

SLEIGH RIDE
First published in 1948, this animated tune was written by Mitchell Parish, a well-regarded Tin Pan Alley

lyricist, and Leroy Anderson, one of the great American masters of light, orchestral music. Arthur Fiedler and the Boston Pops first recorded the song as an instrumental classical piece. The Andrews Sisters released the first known vocal recording in 1950. Other artists such as Ella Fitzgerald, Jo Stafford, Spike Jones, Johnny Mathis, The Ventures, Neil Diamond, Natalie Cole and others have recorded this song.

Arranged and orchestrated by Billy May, "Sleigh Ride" glides along merrily as Karen cajoles you into fun activities of the season.

IT'S CHRISTMAS TIME
Written by Victor Young (who also wrote "When I Fall in Love" on the "Lovelines" CD) and Al Stillman and first published in 1962, "It's Christmas Time" was arranged and orchestrated by Peter Knight. With Richard at the piano and Karen singing, this tune has a baroque feel akin to the treatment of "From this Moment On." Richard's musical and comedic muse Spike Jones performed the medley "It's Christmas Time/Sleep Well Little Children" on his album "Let's Sing a Song of Christmas."

SLEEP WELL, LITTLE CHILDREN
First published in 1956, "Sleep Well, Little Children" was written by Alan Bergman and Leon Klatzkin. Lyricist/songwriter Alan Bergman is well known for his work with wife Marilyn Bergman in music for stage and film, including "The Windmills of Your Mind," "The Way We Were," and "How Do You Keep the Music Playing?" Leon Klatzkin is a composer for feature films and television, including "Rawhide" and "The Wild, Wild West." Karen sings this song tenderly and softly as a lullaby.

HAVE YOURSELF A MERRY LITTLE CHRISTMAS
Along with "The Trolley Song," "Have Yourself a Merry Little Christmas" was immortalized by Judy Garland in the 1944 movie "Meet Me in St. Louis." First published in 1943, it was written by Hugh Martin and Ralph Blane,

both of whom were inducted into the Songwriters Hall of Fame in 1983. The original is a much darker song written about the hope of a better Christmas in the future. "Have Yourself a Merry Little Christmas" is regarded a true torch song.

The original lyrics in part read as follows:

"I know that
In a year we all will be together
If the fates allow
Until then, we'll just have to muddle through somehow
And have ourselves a merry little Christmas now..."

Judy didn't like the tone of the lyrics, so the song was changed to accommodate her.

With arrangement and orchestration by Billy May, Karen brings new life to this song and more optimistic outlook on life with some further revised lyrics.

SANTA CLAUS IS COMING TO TOWN
First published in 1934, "Santa Claus is Coming to Town" was written by Haven Gillespie and J. Fred Coots, both of whom also wrote the pop standard "You Go to My Head." Coots came up with the skeleton of the music for "Santa Claus" in just ten minutes, and Eddie Cantor made it an instant hit on his radio show. This cautionary song has been used in many movies and television shows, including "The Godfather," "Roger and Me," "Home Alone," "The Santa Clause," "Elf," "Fahrenheit 9/11," "Surviving Christmas" and a show of the same name.

Unlike the jazzy version of "Santa Claus is Coming to Town" that the Carpenters originally recorded as a single, the version on this album takes a more traditional choral approach to the song. With Peter Knight doing the arrangement and orchestration, it features the vocals of the Tom Bahler Chorale.

How Tom Bahler came to know the Carpenters is a

story unto itself. During the "Christmas Portrait" sessions, Karen was driving down Highland Avenue toward A&M records. The traffic was heavy when she saw a man do an illegal U-turn in his Porsche convertible. She was surprised to learn the driver was Tom Bahler. Ten years earlier, Tom and his brother John had hired Karen and Richard to promote an upcoming new car called the Ford Maverick. Richard asked Tom (who wrote the song "She's Out of My Life" from Michael Jackson's 1979 album "Off the Wall") to assemble a choir for the Christmas album. Karen would later say the sight of Tom Bahler doing a U-turn, "piqued her interest." From there they began dating. The romance lasted only about a year, but they went their separate ways with a mutual love for each other.

CHRISTMAS SONG
Written by jazz singer/songwriter Mel Tormé and Robert Wells, "The Christmas Song (Chestnuts Roasting on an Open Fire)" is a classic long associated with Nat King Cole, who recorded it first in 1946 with his trio, and then again in 1961 to create his definitive, full-orchestra version.

Arranged and orchestrated by Billy May, this song enjoys a compelling interpretation by Karen with her own special touches, creating for many people yet another classic.

SILENT NIGHT
The German words for what we know as "Silent Night" were originally written by a young priest named Joseph Mohr in 1816, when he was assigned to a pilgrimage church in Mariapfarr, Austria. On December 24, 1818, he requested his friend Franz Gruber in nearby Arnsdorf to add a melody and guitar accompaniment so that it could be sung at Midnight Mass. "Stille Nacht! Heilige Nacht" was heard for the first time in a village church in Oberndorf, Austria. From these humble beginnings the song has evolved into different manifestations, and it is said there exist over 300 translations of the song in the world.

Karen sings this song with simplicity and clarity, and noted that its intrinsic beauty more than compensates what this song lacked in rhythm.

JINGLE BELLS

"Jingle Bells," originally named "One Horse Open Sleigh," was written in 1857 by James Pierpoint. It was originally sung at a Thanksgiving program at his church in Savannah, Georgia, and repeated at Christmas due to its instant popularity. It has become one of the most well-known secular songs around the world, and its lyrics have often been altered in many parodies.

Richard wanted to give "Jingle Bells" a toy-soldier ambiance, and Peter Knight managed to do so with the playful, instrumental passage in the middle of the song.

FIRST SNOWFALL

First published in 1953, "First Snowfall" was written by Paul Francis Webster and Jay Francis Burke. Webster was an Academy and Grammy Award-winning lyricist who also wrote "Secret Love," "Love is a Many-Splendored Thing" and "The Shadow of Your Smile."

The logical juxtaposition of "First Snowball" and "Let it Snow" was another inspiration by Spike Jones to the Carpenters. The Tom Bahler Chorale did an outstanding job sounding like a cold, howling blizzard as the background to Karen's warm, cozy vocal leads.

LET IT SNOW

"Let It Snow" was written by Sammy Cahn and Jule Styne in 1945. A secular song exalting the simple pleasures and coziness of being with loved ones in the midst of inclement wintry weather, it was used in the 1988 Bruce Willis movie "Die Hard."

Karen sings this song with gusto — almost a joyful counterpart to "Rainy Days and Mondays," another song about finding the security of love in an inhospitable environment.

CAROL OF THE BELLS

Lyrics to "Carol of the Bells" were adapted to the original folk music from the Ukraine by Peter Wilhousky in 1936, but the original Ukranian lyrics was entitled "Shchedryk," meaning bountiful, and were sung to celebrate the New Year and tells a story of a swallow flying into a household to sing of wealth that will come with the following spring.

"Carol of the Bells" was suggested by Ray Charles (the choral Ray Charles, aka Charles Raymond Offenberg) for Richard to perform as a piano solo when the Carpenters were guests at the Perry Como Christmas show three or four years prior to this album.

MERRY CHRISTMAS DARLING

The Carpenters' first attempt at Christmas music was with the delightful "Merry Christmas Darling." The lyrics were written in 1946 by Frank Pooler. Pooler was the choir director at California State University, Long Beach, where Karen and Richard were both part of the choir. In 1966, at Pooler's request, Richard composed the music for this tender ballad, which has been a hit every Christmas since its release in 1970. This is the only other song arranged and orchestrated by Richard on this album. This was Karen's favorite Christmas song because of its direct connection to Frank Pooler and her brother Richard. The version which appeared on "Christmas Portrait" is a re-recording with a new mix by Richard and a newly recorded vocal by Karen.

I'LL BE HOME FOR CHRISTMAS

"I'll Be Home for Christmas" was written by Kim Gannon, Walter Kent and Buck Ram. Bing Crosby popularized it in 1943, in the midst of World War II when soldiers and civilians alike were touched by this song. Other crooners like Frank Sinatra subsequently recorded it. In December 1965, astronauts Frank Borman and James Lovell requested NASA to play this song on their completion of the first US space rendezvous, setting a record for the longest flight in the

US space program.

Karen sang this song with a great depth of feeling and yearning, hinting at a hope and promise that may never be fulfilled as the song ends with *"I'll be home for Christmas ... if only in my dreams."*

CHRIST IS BORN
"Christ is Born" was written by Ray Charles (again, not the singer/pianist Ray Charles Robinson, whose stage name was also Ray Charles) and Domenico Bartolucci. First copyrighted in 1934, "Christ is Born" has been performed by other artists with the likes of Perry Como (Richard Carpenter first heard the song on the 1968 "The Perry Como Christmas Album." Karen and Richard had originally learned this song from their school days where it was performed with two choirs, totaling about 80 voices.

WINTER WONDERLAND
Dick Smith and Felix Bernard wrote "Winter Wonderland." Originally published in 1934, this peppy tune received high acclaim, especially the versions by the Andrews Sisters and Perry Como.

A verse not included in the Carpenters' version is:

"When it snows, ain't it thrilling,
Though your nose gets a chilling
We'll frolic and play, the Eskimo way
Walking in a winter wonderland."

SILVER BELLS
Jay Livingston and Ray Evans wrote "Silver Bells," first copyrighted in 1950. The Carpenters performed this tune in the Spike Jones-inspired tradition, with all the trimmings and obligatory silliness thrown in.

WHITE CHRISTMAS
A Russian-Jewish immigrant with little direct experience of the holiday, Irving Berlin wrote "White Christmas" in early 1940. So confident was he that this

was the best song he had ever written, he even dared to say this was the best song that ANYONE has ever written. This song was introduced in the 1942 musical "Holiday Inn" by Bing Crosby and Marjorie Reynolds, and went on to win an Academy Award for Best Song. The feeling of homesickness resonated with listeners during the World War II era, and this song went to the top of US music charts in 1942, 1945 and 1946 during the respective holiday seasons. The most familiar version of "White Christmas" was recorded in 1947 after the original master was damaged from frequent use. "White Christmas" was reprised in another movie of the same name, starring Bing Crosby, Danny Kaye, Rosemary Clooney and Vera-Ellen in 1954. The 2007 Guinness Book of Records lists Crosby's recording as the biggest-selling single of all time with an estimated 50 million copies sold in singles and 100 million in total. ASCAP lists "White Christmas" as the most performed holiday song in recorded history with over 500 versions in 25 languages (The 2009 Guinness Book of Records has since listed Elton John's 1997 recording of "Candle in the Wind" [tribute to Princess Diana] as the biggest selling single of all-time).

The introduction, which points to the incongruity of a wintry Christmas in sunny Los Angeles against an idealized snowy wonderland of youth, was used as a transition from spoken dialog into the song, but was subsequently dropped by Irving Berlin and remained unfamiliar to most audiences. The Carpenters resurrected the introduction which goes:

"The sun is shining
The grass is green
The orange and palm trees sway
There's never been such a day
In Beverly Hills, L.A.
But it's December the 24th
And I'm longing to be up North..."

Karen said Bing Crosby was her "favorite human," and she said modestly she hoped she did justice to this song.

AVE MARIA

The text to "Ave Maria" is one of the most popular Catholic prayers, composed of two distinct parts, a Scriptural part from as early as the Fourth or Fifth Century and an intercessory part from the 15th Century where two endings are found. The music to this version of "Ave Maria," which is not as well-known as the version by Franz Schubert, was written by Johann Sebastian Bach for the first prelude from the Well-Tempered Clavier and adapted by Charles Gounod in the 19th Century.

The Carpenters had kept both versions of music in mind when recording, but due to time limitations, a decision had to be made, and the road less traveled was taken. According to Karen, the Bach-Gounod version was "just a touch classier." The recording of the choral backup was for a while misplaced and thought to be lost, so Karen ended up singing solo without choral accompaniment on the mix in this album. However, the simplicity, purity and immediacy of the sound perhaps contribute even more to that "chill" factor.

Made in America (click here to purchase)
Released: June 16, 1981
Producer: Richard Carpenter
Arrangements: Richard Carpenter
Orchestration: Richard Carpenter, Peter Knight, Paul Riser
Conductor: Frank Pooler (Because We Are in Love)
Director: Ron Hicklin (Because We Are In Love)
Lead Vocals: Karen Carpenter
Background Vocals: Karen Carpenter, Richard Carpenter, Carolyn Dennis, Stephanie Spruill, Maxine Waters Willard, OK Chorale
Drums: Ron Tutt, Larrie Londin, John Robinson, Karen Carpenter
Percussion: Paulinho DeCosta, Peter Limonick, Karen Carpenter, Bob Conti
Congas: Jerry Steinholtz
Keyboards: Richard Carpenter
Electric Guitar: Tony Peluso, Tim May

Acoustic Guitar: Tim May, Dennis Budimir, Fred Tackett
Steel Guitar: Jay Dee Maness
Bass: Joe Osborn
Tenor Sax: Tom Scott
Oboe: Earl Dumler
Harmonica: Tom Morgan
Harp: Gayle Levant
Synthesizer: Daryl Dragon, Ian Underwood
Concertmaster (Lead Violin): Jimmy Getzoff, Jerry Vinci
Engineer: Roger Young and Ray Gerhardt
Assistant Engineer: Dave Iveland
Mastering Engineer: Bernie Grundman
Mix-down Engineer: Roger Young
Mix-down Assistant: Stewart Whitmore
Mixed at SoundLabs and A&M Recording Studios
Art Direction: Chuck Beeson, Jeff Ayeroff
Album Design: Lynn Robb
Illustration: David Williardson, Willardson & White Inc.
Photography: John Engstead
Special Thanks: Gary Sims, Pat Peters, Ron Gorow, John Bettis, Jules Chaikin, Herb Alpert, Jerry Moss, Gil and the entire A&M Family
Chart Positions: US #52/ UK #12/ Japan #44/ Australia #50
Certifications: Silver (UK)
Singles: I Believe You Touch Me When We're Dancing, (Want You) Back in My Life Again, Those Good Old Dreams, Beechwood 4-5789
Rick Henry's Rating: 6.9

"Made in America" was received with mixed reviews and viewpoints. Some fans believed the album to be one of Carpenters' best, and others found it to be a disappointment. Some fans commented that although Karen was still in good vocal form, she did not have the same verve as she did in previous recordings. Some of the songs found Karen singing beyond her range of comfort. Many reviewers took note that Carpenters were back in familiar territory but lacked the cutting edge of their earlier works. One reviewer had commented that the music and vocals sounded air-brushed. "Made in America" was Carpenters' attempt to recapture the magic of their previous work. "Those Good Old Dreams" is an enchanting, upbeat number which reviewers called a rehash

"On Top of the World." "Because We Are in Love" was an attempt to repeat the brilliance of "We've Only Just Begun" by introducing a new wedding song for a new generation, yet lacking the grandeur of the former. "Beechwood 4-5789" was an attempt to emulate the super-successful "Please Mr. Postman" but with much less impact and energy. Even the guitar solo in "Beechwood" (which was very good) did not stand up to Tony Peluso's electrifying solo in "Postman." "When You've Got What It Takes" contains one of the most inspirational lyrics of any song recorded by Carpenters, but loses some of its emotional impact from the redundancy of the musical arrangement.

Then there's the issue of the album cover; the illustration and design of the cover is professionally rendered. Yet, somehow, it gave this extremely talented duo a cartoon image instead of a serious, musician image. It pushed the Carpenters right back into the "sugary-sweet" image they had so much wanted to escape in the 70's.

Despite its downfalls "Made in America" does contain many redeeming moments. First and foremost is Karen Carpenter's silky voice. Karen gives us her usual, top-notch vocal performance on "Made in America." The music itself is, as always, very well-produced and performed with the utmost of professionalism as we find on all Carpenters albums. Songs like "Those Good Old Dreams," "Somebody's Been Lyin'" and "(Want You) Back in My Life Again" are delightful tunes as good as any in the Carpenters catalog. "I Believe You" is one of the album's highlights featuring a soulful and powerful reading by Karen Carpenter. The most appealing aspect of the album is its upbeat 80's sound in songs like "Touch Me When We're Dancing" and "(Want You) Back in My Life Again." This is a sound Carpenters most likely would have honed and perfected throughout the 80's had Karen lived. Richard Carpenter described the album as being "a very American sound, even more so, a California sound."

To promote the album Karen and Richard did a 1981 promotional tour of television performances throughout the US, South America, Europe and Japan. They appeared on shows such as Good Morning America (US), The Merv Griffin Show

(US), Toppop Show (Holland), Nationwide (UK), Program 80'
Generation (Brazil) and several others.

"Made in America" charted in less countries than any other
Carpenters album that was released while Karen was alive
(with the exception of "Christmas Portrait"). This was to be
Carpenters big comeback. Instead, the album fizzled out as
quickly as it was released. To be certain, the album contained
some well-crafted songs, but there was nothing close to the
level of "Rainy Days and Mondays," "A Song for You," "This
Masquerade," "Only Yesterday" or "Solitaire". It looked like the
big comeback for Carpenters was going to have to wait for a
future release. Sadly, though, Karen Carpenter passed away
one year and seven months after the release of "Made in
America," and this ended up being their final studio album.
Some have said that Karen Carpenter deserved to have her
final album be a blockbuster instead of a lackluster.

All-in-all "Made in America" is an engaging addition to the
Carpenters body of work.

1.   Those Good Old Dreams (Richard Carpenter / John
Bettis) 4:12
        "Those Good Old Dreams" seemed like the appropriate
        way to open the album. The line *"Like an old love song,
        gone for much too long"* brings to mind that Carpenters'
        brand of "love songs" had been gone for a while, and
        now they're back with a new sound and a sense of
        optimism and excitement *("No more dark horizons, only
        blue... It's a new day for those good old dreams")*.

        Instantly the magic of that Carpenters sound is revived
        with "Those Good Old Dreams" and quickly becomes a
        fan favorite. The song captures the same sort of
        country-tinged, sunshiny-cheer as found in their classic
        "Top of the World." "Those Good Old Dreams" has
        enjoyed a fair amount of club play in country and
        western dance clubs throughout the US where it is a
        popular song for the two-step.

        "Those Good Old Dreams" was released as a single on
        November 5, 1981, and was the third single from "Made

in America" (actually, the fourth if you count "I Believe You"). Fans and some industry insiders expected this song to become a Top 40 hit. Sadly, it only reached #63 on the US chart and failed to chart anywhere else in the world. However, this was a slight improvement from the previous single "(Want You) Back in My Life Again" which made it to #72.

- **Note from Rick Henry:** *This is one of the few songs from "Made In America" that I truly love.*

2.   Strength of a Woman (Phyllis Brown / Juanita Curiel)
3:59

This song has an interesting background. It was first recorded in 1980 by R&B Jazz singer Eloise Laws for her album "Eloise Laws." Carpenters' recording is very similar in style and arrangement to Laws' recording.

The song's writers also have an interesting history. Phyllis Brown got her start in music at a very young age having recorded a single for the Hollywood, CA, label Rainbo Records called "Why" with "Oh Baby" on the B-side. Brown was only 16 when she recorded this northern, soul single. Other than "Strength of a Woman," she is also known for her song "Lookin for a Lovin'" which has been recorded by Phyllis Hyman, Dorothy Moore and Ann Peebles. Juanita Curiel (born in Mexico and raised in Las Vegas, NV,) was a member of the R&B trio Hot, who had a Top 10 hit in 1977 with "Angel in Your Arms." Juanita also provided vocals on the song "Just a Feeling" on Stanley Clarke's 1979 album "I Wanna Play for You."

Carpenters' recording of the song retained much of the same jazz- influenced R&B tones as found on Eloise Laws' recording. Although where Laws' vocal performance was outwardly soul-filled (ala Donna Summer) Karen Carpenter's performance was more introspective giving the song a meditative, melancholy about it. This is one of a few Carpenters tunes that include background vocals other than Karen and

Richard, featuring the vocal works of Carolyn Dennis, Stephanie Spruill and Maxine Waters Willard.

3. <u>(Want You) Back in My Life Again (Kerry Chater /Chris Christian)</u>3:40
This was the second single released from "Made in America" (third if you count "I Believe You"). The song was one of their least successful singles reaching only #72 on the US charts (and not charting anywhere else in the world). Quite a few people were expecting this lighthearted dance-pop tune to sell better than it did.

Daryl Dragon (The Captain and Tennille) and Ian Underwood (from Frank Zappa's Mothers of Invention) are credited for the synthesizer programming on this song. Richard Carpenter is a huge fan of Frank Zappa, and, ironically, it is with this lightweight (yet infectiously-catchy) tune that he finally is able to work with someone affiliated with Zappa.

Songwriter Chris Christian is a successful Christian music artist and producer who has recorded more than 15 solo Christian albums and has also had a few, pop hits including the 1981 Top 40 hit "I Want You, I Need You." Christian produced Amy Grant's 1977 debut album "Amy Grant" and has said that Carpenters are the influence he (and Brown Bannister) called upon when working on Amy's albums. His rendition of "(Want You) Back in My Life Again" is included on his album "Harbour" which was released in 2000. He was very excited when he heard Carpenters decided to record the song. To this day it's one of his favorite tracks along with the song Elvis recorded. Elvis recorded Chris Christian's "Love Song of the Year" in 1975.

- **Note from Rick Henry:** *I really enjoy the upbeat nature of this tune. I always enjoy it when Carpenters include synthesizer sounds in their music. It's a dimension that adds a little something different from their standard sound.*

4.   When You've Got What It Takes (Bill Lane / Roger
Nichols) 3:41

Fans of this song recognize it for its optimistic lyric. The
song is an anthem of feeling good about yourself and
letting it show.

Beyond the "feel good" lyric, the song never really
becomes anything more than a pleasant album track.
Toward the end, the song becomes a tad bit long-
winded with its repetitious chorus.

The songwriting team of Bill Lane and Roger Nichols is
best remembered for the song "Times of Your Life"
which was a Top 10 hit for Paul Anka in 1975. Of course,
Roger Nichols is the same person who wrote several
mega-hits with Paul Williams such as "We've Only Just
Begun," "Let Me Be the One" and "I Won't Last a Day
Without You." Bill Lane is a renowned studio musician
having played French horn for several artists including
Judy Collins, Kenny Rogers, Michael Bolton, David
Foster and Diana Krall. Lane has also done work as a
music producer and engineer.

5.   Somebody's Been Lyin' (Carole Bayer Sager / Burt
Bacharach) 4:25

Karen performs this intimate tune to perfection. Her
vocal leads one to feel as if she is singing from personal
experience of a romance that once was and could have
been. Richard's subdued arrangement quietly and
calmly conveys the realization and heartbreak of the
song's lyric.

"Somebody's Been Lyin'" is a highlight on the album, a
favorite amongst fans and one that is well-received by
critics. It was used as the B-side on the single "(Want
You) Back in My Life Again."

Lyricist Carole Bayer Sager married Burt Bacharach in
1982 (a year after "Made In America" was released).
Bayer Sager's first big hit was The Mindbenders 1965
hit "A Groovy Kind of Love" which has been covered by
an endless stream of recording artists. Other songs she's

written and/or co-written include Melissa Manchester's "Don't Cry Out Loud," Carly Simon's "Nobody Does It Better," Leo Sayer's "When I Need You" and Rita Coolidge's "I'd Rather Leave While I'm in Love." She's written a good amount of classic hits with Burt Bacharach, including Christopher Cross' "Arthur's Theme (Best That I Can Do)," Patti Labelle's "On My Own," Neil Diamond's "Heartlight" and the mega-hit "That's What Friends Are For." In 1977, she had her own hit single with "You're Movin' Out Today" (co-written with Bette Midler) and reached #69 on the US singles chart. Carole Bayer Sager's recording of "Somebody's Been Lyin'" appears on her 1981 album "Sometimes Late at Night."

6. <u>I Believe You (Dick and Don Addrisi)</u> 3:54
This is a perfect example of the soulfulness in Karen's voice. Though the musical arrangement and orchestration is pure pop, Karen's vocal is filled with yearning intonations of soul that we do not find in many of her earlier performances. That's not to say that Karen wasn't soulful in her earlier performances. To be certain, Karen has always had a certain degree of soulfulness in her voice, but this time around it seems that Karen may have taken note of the vocal styles of Carmen McCrae or Nancy Wilson. With her solo album, Karen further delved into the soulful side of her voice.

"I Believe You" was released on October 20, 1978, two years and eight months before "Made In America" was released. The song was originally recorded for an album that was to be released in 1979. Had the album been released it most likely would have included "I Believe You," "Thank You for the Music," "Dancing in the Street," "Look to Your Dreams," "Honolulu City Lights," "The Rainbow Connection," "Leave Yesterday Behind," "Where Do I Go from Here," "When I Fall in Love," "Slow Dance," "Little Girl Blue" and "Prime Time Love."

"I Believe You" was released with a minimum of fanfare or promotion (even die-hard fans almost missed the release of this one). All of Carpenters' previous singles (with the exception of "Goofus") had placed on the charts in half a dozen or more countries around the world. "I Believe You" only charted in the US at #68 and Canada at #81. At this point in time it was their least-successful single. Some critics took note of the almost "Christmassy" sound of the song, which would make sense as the song was recorded during the same recording sessions as "Christmas Portrait."

Soul singer Dorothy Moore released the song in 1977 and had a hit with it making it to #27 in the US and #20 in the UK. Moore is best remembered for her 1976 hit "Misty Blue" which was a Top Five hit in the US, UK, Australia, Canada, New Zealand and South Africa. Barbara Mandrell also recorded the song for her 1978 album "Moods," which is her best-selling album to date.

Songwriters Dick and Don Addrisi (brothers) are best remembered for writing the mega-hit "Never My Love" which was a Top Three hit for the Association in 1967. The Fifth Dimension took "Never My Love" into the Top 15 in 1971, and the Swedish rock group Blue Swede took the song into the Top 10 in 1974. The Addrisi Brothers also wrote the theme song for the early 70's television show "Nanny and the Professor." Along with their success as songwriters they recorded their own hit songs including "We've Got to Get it On Again" #25 in 1972 and "Slow Dancin' Don't Turn Me On" #20 in 1977.

- **Note from Rick Henry:** *I first heard this song in December 1978, while driving in the canyon -- it was late at night, and I was on my way home from a friend's house. I was caught off-guard because I had no idea that a new Carpenters recording had been released. I was a few days shy of 19 years old and was not really paying much attention to new Carpenters releases. I went to my local music store the very next day and bought the single.*

7. Touch Me When We're Dancing (Terry Skinner / Ken Bell / J.L. Wallace (3:20)

"Touch Me When We're Dancing" was released in May 1981 (a month before "Made in America"). The game plan was that this single would be Carpenters' big comeback. As history would have it, that's not the way it turned out. The song received moderate airplay, but the record-buying public did not go for it. It managed to make it to #16 on the US chart (which was not too impressive considering this was their comeback release). The song charted in only two other countries in the world: #22 in New Zealand and #78 in Australia, then it quickly disappeared. This was the last US Top 20 hit for Carpenters.

The song is a pleasant number featuring some nice guitar work by Tony Peluso and an engaging, sax solo by Tom Scott. Richard Carpenter recognized that producing a stronger, rhythmic sound would give the song a more contemporary feel as Carpenters moved into the 80's. This was ably accomplished with the arrangement of a rhythmic trio consisting of Paulinho DaCosta on percussion, Larrie London on drums and Joe Osborn on bass guitar. Carolyn Dennis joined Karen and Richard on background vocals (one of the few songs that includes vocals other than Karen and Richard's).

This song was originally recorded and released in 1979 by a band from Alabama named Bama. Their version made it to #86 on the US singles chart. The band members of Bama are songwriters Terry Skinner, Ken Bell and J.L. Wallace. This trio also wrote the hit song "Even the Nights are Better" which was a huge hit for Air Supply in 1982. They have also written songs recorded by Melissa Manchester, Reba McEntire, Peabo Bryson, Oakridge Boys, Roberta Flack and many others.

"Touch Me When We're Dancing" has also been recorded by country band Alabama in 1986 and took the song to #1 on the country music charts. Charly McClain and Mickey Gilley recorded and released the song on their 1984 collaboration album "It Takes Believers." Finally, jazz R&B vocalist Charlotte Doreen Small recorded the song for her 2007 album "More."

8. <u>When It's Gone (It's Just Gone) (Randy Handley)</u> 5:01
Karen's spirited yet heartrending performance of this
song combined with Jay Dee Maness' steel guitar gives
this song a laid-back feel of broken dreams and
heartbreak. It has that Southern California sunset feel
and sound to it.

Performed and arranged extremely well, "When It's
Gone (It's Just Gone)" was used as the flipside to the
single "Those Good Old Dreams." These two songs made
a great combination, as they both have that touch-of-
country music which suits the Carpenters very well.

Songwriter Randy Handley wrote this song in 1980 and
was first recorded by Charlie Rich in 1980 for his album
"Once a Drifter." Randy Handley also wrote "Stolen
Night" recorded by Joey Scarbury for his "Greatest
American Hero" album in 1981. Diana Ross recorded
Handley's "Still in Love" which appeared on her 1982
"Silk Degrees" album.

9. <u>Beechwood 4-5789 (Marvin Gaye / George Gordy /
William "Mickey" Stevenson)</u> 3:06
This Motown remake was the fifth and final single
release from "Made in America." It also has the
distinction of being the last single released while Karen
was still alive. The single was only a moderate hit for
Carpenters in the US, reaching just #74, but in New
Zealand it was a sizable hit making it to #10. Other than
the US and New Zealand, the song did not chart
anywhere else.

One of the highlights of this song is the great guitar solo,
which is actually performed by Tim May (surprisingly, it
is not Tony Peluso).

A music video for the song was shot at A&M Records'
Chaplin Stage. It was a nostalgic 60's video set in a soda
shop complete with jukebox and teenage dancers doing
popular dance routines of the day. Then the video
switches over to a female's bedroom with pink walls

and an oversized, pink Princess telephone. Karen looks obviously thin in the video but seems to really enjoy herself. Fans have mixed views of this video; some love it, but many say the video is somewhat on the "corny" side.

One of the song's co-writers is the incomparable Marvin Gaye. We all know Marvin Gaye for his many hits which include, "How Sweet It Is (To Be Loved by You," "You're All I Need to Get By," "I Heard It Through the Grapevine," "What's Going On," "Mercy, Mercy Me," "Let's Get It On," "Got to Give It Up," and many, many others.

The Marvelettes made this song a hit in 1962 and took it to #17. This was the second Marvelettes tune Carpenters covered; the first is "Please Mr. Postman."

- **Note from Rick Henry:** *I have always enjoyed the guitar solo on this (although it's not as great as the solo on "Please Mr. Postman"). I was surprised when I learned Tony Peluso did not play the solo. I had always assumed it was Peluso. Tim May did a great job and sounds quite a bit like Peluso on this song.*

10. <u>Because We Are in Love (The Wedding Song) (Richard Carpenter / John Bettis)</u> 5:04
On August 31, 1980, Karen Carpenter was married to Thomas Burris. Her wedding was a lavish event held in the Crystal Room of the Beverly Hills Hotel. Upon Karen's request, Richard and songwriting partner John Bettis wrote "Because We Are in Love (The Wedding Song)" which was played during the wedding ceremony. Richard Carpenter's vision was to write the song in a sweeping, show-tune style in order to capture the glee of the gala event. Famed conductor/orchestrator, Peter Knight, was flown in from England to orchestrate this piece in time for the wedding. The song was played as Karen walked down the aisle.

Former Long Beach University tutor, (and now Carpenters lifelong friend) Frank Pooler, was invited to conduct the OK Chorale for the recording on the album.

The lyrics (written by John Bettis) acutely reflected Karen's emotions -- both hopeful and uncertain. By the time the album was released (nine and a half months after her wedding), her marriage was already faltering. On the day of her passing in 1983 she had plans to visit with a divorce lawyer. She was still married to Tom Burris when she died, although they had been separated for about a year.

"Because We Are in Love (The Wedding Song)" was the first glimpse at what was to come on "Made in America," first, when it was played at Karen's wedding and second, as it was used for the B-side of the single "Touch Me When We're Dancing."

Voice of the Heart (click here to purchase)
Released: October 18, 1983
Producer: Richard Carpenter
Arrangements: Richard Carpenter, Peter Knight (Look to Your Dreams)
Lead Vocals: Karen Carpenter
Background Vocals: Karen Carpenter, Richard Carpenter, The OK Chorale (under the direction of Ron Hicklin, conducted by Dick Bolk)
Drums: Ron Tutt, Ed Greene, Larrie Londin
Percussion: Paulinho DaCosta, Peter Limonick
Keyboards: Richard Carpenter
Electric Guitar: Tony Peluso
Acoustic Guitar: Tim May, Tony Peluso, Dennis Budimir, Fred Tackett
Steel Guitar: Jay Dee Maness
Bass: Joe Osborn, Chuck Del'Monico
Tenor Sax: John Phillips, Tom Scott
Oboe: Earl Dumler
English Horn: Earl Dumler
Flute: Sheridon Stokes, Tom Scott
Flugelhorn: Chuck Findley, Ron Gorow, John Audino
Recorders: Sheridon Stokes

Trumpet: Chuck Findley
Harp: Gayle Levant
Synthesizer: Shaun Furlong
Concertmaster (Lead Violin): Jimmy Getzoff
Engineer: Roger "Mingo" Young
Assistant Engineer: Robert De La Garza
Mastering Engineer: Bernie Grundman
Mix-down Engineer: Roger Young
Mix-down Assistant: Robert De La Garza, David Cole, Robin Laine
Recorded at A&M Recording Studios
Mixed at A&M Recording Studios, Capitol Recording Studios and The Village Recorder
Contractor: Jules Chaikin
Art Direction: Chuck Beeson
Photography: Claude Mougin (front cover), Larry Williams (back cover), Annie Liebovitz (inner sleeve)
Special Thanks: Ron Gorow, John Bettis, Roger Young, Don Hahn, Mimi Thomas, all the guys in the shop: Ken, Gary, Bill, Karl; Werner Wolfen, Herb, Jerry and the entire A&M family
Personal Management: Jerry Weintraub
Chart Positions: #6 UK, #16 US, #41 Japan, #54 Australia
Certifications: Gold (US), Gold (UK)
Singles: Make Believe It's Your First Time, Your Baby Doesn't Love You Anymore, Now
Rick Henry's Rating: 7.2

"Voice of the Heart" was the first album released after Karen's untimely death due to heart failure stemming from Anorexia Nervosa. Many fans call "Voice of the Heart" the Carpenters 11th studio album, but in reality it is not a studio album as only two of the songs were recorded for the album. The rest of the songs are collected from various periods of Carpenters recording career. "Voice of the Heart" is Carpenters first compilation of previously unreleased material. To date Carpenters have released three compilations of previously unreleased material, the other two being "Lovelines" (1989) and "As Time Goes By" (2000).

"Voice of the Heart" had been released onto a public that had fallen out of love with the Carpenters. It did, however, chart and sell better than the previous album "Made in America," but

300,000 US sales hardly set the music world on fire ("Made in America" sold only 150,000 US copies).

One music critic stated that "Voice of the Heart" was not the most compelling work released by Carpenters, but it was an appropriate and poignant reminder of how Karen Carpenter enriched the world with her graceful voice.

A month after Karen's passing Richard returned to the recording studio to work on "Voice of the Heart." He felt he owed it to his sister's memory to complete this album. He said, "I know she would have wanted it this way." Richard wanted this album to be Karen's.

Here is a listing of the recording dates of each song on this compilation: "You're Enough" (1981), "Now" (1982), "You're Baby Doesn't Love You Anymore" (1980), "Two Lives" (1980), "Make Believe It's Your First Time" (1980), "At the End of a Song" (1980), "Look to Your Dreams" (1978), "Ordinary Fool" (1976), "Sailing on the Tide" (1975), "Prime Time Love" (not certain, possibly 1980).

1. <u>Now (Roger Nichols / Dean Pitchford)</u> 3:51
Legions of Carpenters fans hold "Now" in high regard for many reasons; most predominantly because it is the last song Karen ever recorded. During this time period Karen was living in New York getting medical treatment for complications brought on from Anorexia Nervosa. In April 1982, she decided to take a break from her treatment and flew back to California for a short visit. She spent some time in the studio laying down a "work vocal" for "Now," which would be used for the purpose of piecing together the instrumental track of the song. The intent would be for Karen to come back into the studio to record a final vocal to be used for the song. Sadly, that final vocal was never recorded. What is included on "Voice of the Heart" is the "work vocal" with orchestration and a steamy, sax solo added in 1983. Although the "work vocal" is not up to par with Karen's finest work, it does, however, reveal the fact that Karen's voice remained intact even during the worst of her illness.

With its mournful feel "Now" seemed tailor-made for Karen's voice accentuating the built-in sadness in Karen's voice. Although the song has a melancholy feel about it the lyric itself is warmly optimistic, *"Now, now when it rains I don't feel cold. Now that I have your hand to hold. The winds might blow through me, but I don't care. There's no harm in thunder if you are there."*

"Now" was the third single release from the album though it did not chart. The song, nonetheless, has remained a favorite amongst die-hard fans.

Songwriter Roger Nichols is best remembered for the many hits he co-wrote with Paul Williams ("We've Only Just Begun," "Rainy Days and Mondays," "Let Me Be the One," "I Won't Last a Day Without You," "I Kept on Loving You," "The Rainbow Connection" and several others). Nichols recorded an album for A&M Records in 1968 called "Roger Nichols and the Small Circle of Friends"; the album did not chart, but was his pathway to meeting Paul Williams.

Dean Pitchford co-wrote "Now" with Roger Williams. Dean Pitchford became one of the most prolific and popular songwriters of the 80's co-writing countless hits including "Footloose," "Almost Paradise," "Holding Out for a Hero" and "Let's Hear It for the Boy" from the "Footloose" soundtrack. From the "Fame" soundtrack he co-wrote "Fame," "Red Light," "I Sing the Body Electric" and "Miles from Here." He also co-wrote Melissa Manchester's "You Should Hear How They Talk About You," "Change of Heart" and "Make Me Lose Control" both by Eric Carmen and "Dancing in the Sheets" by Shalamar. Musicians from all across the musical spectrum including Peter Cetera, Jennifer Holliday, Cliff Richard, Whitney Houston, Cher, Kim Carnes, Dolly Parton, Hilary Duff, Barbra Streisand, Roger Daltrey and Louise Mandrell have recorded Pitchford's songs.

2.   Sailing on the Tide (Tony Peluso / John Bettis) 4:24

This song was co-written by Carpenters' guitarist, Tony Peluso. "Sailing on the tide" was recorded in 1975 during the "Horizon" sessions, but did not make the album. No need to feel bad for Tony, as one of his songs did make it on "Horizon," that song, of course, is the ever-popular "Happy."

During the recording sessions for "Horizon" Carpenters had a particularly tough time bringing this song together and decided to put it aside in order to proceed with other songs.

"Sailing on the Tide" contains a range of good-time, upbeat feelings including flourishes of both acoustic and electric guitar. Of course, the guitar has its presence in this song being written by Tony Peluso.

One of the most prominent attractions in the song is the fun tempo change in the middle, where Tony's electric guitar goes wild and swirling, synthesized-percussive effects appear.

Karen's vocal is easygoing and undemanding remaining completely within her lower range. This makes for a very appealing performance by her and brings about that relaxing, Southern California sort of sound.

With its extra touches and fancy frills of summery, sunny sounds "Sailing on the Tide" is well-liked by fans that call the song one of the Carpenters' happiest-sounding songs. One fan said the song "Makes me feel happy with the tropical island imagery and a relaxing, yet upbeat feel."

"Sailing on the Tide" was used as the B-side to "Your Baby Doesn't Love You Anymore" which was released as a single on January 31, 1984.

- **Note from Rick Henry:** *I am particularly fond of this song for its feel-good nature. I also like it because I am a huge fan of Tony Peluso's work with Carpenters. He is my favorite Carpenters band-member.*

3.   <u>You're Enough (Richard Carpenter / John Bettis)</u> 3:47
"You're Enough" and "Now" were the only two songs on this compilation which were actually recorded for the album that would have been released in 1983 had Karen lived. The rest of the songs are outtakes from previous recording sessions, primarily from "Made in America."

"You're Enough" was recorded during the same April 1982 session as "Now," but it was recorded a few days before "Now." It's nice to hear the relaxed direction in which Carpenters were moving with songs like "You're Enough," although with only two songs recorded in 1982, it's hard to tell where they would have gone with the other songs. Knowing Carpenters, they most likely would have given us a nice variety of different styles as they always did with each album.

The song's arrangement is simplistic and charming; it would have been a good fit on the serenely-paced "A Kind of Hush" album. Karen delivers a warm, downbeat vocal performance in which she remains within her lower range quite comfortably. Karen is best when she keeps within her comfort zone. It's that lower voice that makes her almost irresistible.

"You're Enough" is one of four Carpenter/Bettis originals included on "Voice of the Heart." This is the most Carpenter/Bettis tunes on one album since 1975's "Horizon." Even on "Horizon" two of the original tunes are the bookend pieces: "Aurora" and "Eventide."

4.   <u>Make Believe It's Your First Time (Bob Morrison /Johnny Wilson)</u>4:07
Originally Karen recorded this song in 1980 when she was working on her solo album. The recording that appears on "Voice of the Heart" is an entirely different rendition recorded in 1981 during the "Made in America" sessions. The solo recording contained a noticeably, more intimate and richer-toned delivery from Karen.

When it came time to begin work on "Made in America" Richard felt "Make Believe It's Your First Time" was one of the stronger songs from Karen's solo project. He got in touch with the songwriters and had them write a bridge, which was not in Karen's original version. Richard composed an elaborate arrangement including more instruments in the mix. Some say the arrangement is overdone. Many have critiqued the addition of the OK Chorale, on backup vocals, as being a distraction to Karen's lead vocal. When it came time to release "Made in America" it was decided not to use "Make Believe It's Your First Time." Karen's vocal on this recording is one of her finest "work leads" of any that have been released. A work lead is a vocal that is recorded solely for the purpose of being a guide for recording the music tracks. Usually work leads are re-recorded and fine-tuned for the final release. Karen never did a final vocal for this song.

The song was the first single released from the album managing to only generate minimal attention having reached #101 in the US, #60 in the UK and #80 in Australia.

Songwriter Bob Morrison is known for having written or co-written some of country music's biggest hits including "The River's Too Wide" recorded in 1974, Barbara Mandrell's 1976 hit "Midnight Angel," Reba McEntire's 1980 Top 10 country hit "(Lift Me) Up to Heaven." He is best remembered for co-writing Kenny Rogers' 1979 Grammy Award winning hit "You Decorated My Life" and the classic Urban Cowboy track "Lookin' for Love" performed by Johnny Lee.

Johnny Wilson, the song's other co-writer, has written a few songs recorded by country music stars Red Sovine and CW McCall.

"Make Believe It's Your First Time" was predominantly written as a country song which found its audience with the adult contemporary crowd when it was recorded and released in 1979 by Bobby Vinton, who took the song to #78 in the US. Country singer Charly McClain recorded a charming version of the song, which ended up on her 1980 album "Who's Cheatin' Who."

- **Note from Rick Henry:** *I do enjoy the rendition of this song on "Voice of the Heart," but much prefer Karen's solo version. I find her vocal on that version to be much more intimate, and the pared-down musical arrangement suits her voice better.*

5.   Two Lives (Mark Terrence Jordan) 4:35
"Two Lives" is another one of those songs recorded in 1978 during the "Christmas Portrait" sessions. Karen's vocal on this song once again is a work lead. Her vocal is mostly above average; however, it is not her most convincing or strongest performance. Although the song is on the whole unremarkable and doesn't really go anywhere, it is a charming addition to "Voice of the Heart" and includes a fine performance on pedal steel guitar by Jay Dee Maness. Maness appears on several other songs by Carpenters dating as far back as 1973's "Now & Then" album.

Mark Terrence Jordan (who wrote the song) is a multi-instrumentalist who plays guitar, organ, synthesizer and, primarily, keyboards and piano. He has appeared on recordings by Dave Mason, Van Morrison, Buddy Guy, Nicolette Larson, Big Al Downing, The Judds, Taj Mahal, Leo Sayer, Carly Simon, Bonnie Raitt and a host of others. He has written or co-written songs which have been recorded by Tom Jones, Player and Color Me Badd. "Two Lives" is one of Jordan's most popular songs having been recorded by several artists including Bonnie Raitt for her 1977 album "Sweet Forgiveness" and R&B jazz singer Randy Crawford on her 1981 album "Sweet Combination." Bill Medley (of the Righteous Brothers) recorded the song and included it on his 2007 album "Damn Near Righteous."

6.   At the End of a Song (Richard Carpenter / John Bettis) 3:42

This downbeat lyric written by John Bettis could rightfully mirror the feelings Karen had in 1981, as her marriage to Tom Burris was faltering. John Bettis always seemed to capture the emotions of both Karen and Richard with his lyrics, as if they were actually written by Karen and/or Richard themselves.

With Latin-flavored guitar styles by Tim May and Jay Dee Maness and Richard Carpenter's manipulation of the keyboards to give it a marimba type sound, this song has a somewhat Spanish flair to it.

This 1981 "Made in America" outtake suffers from a lazy sort of drag. But with its pleasant feel and Karen's always excellent vocal, it does add a nice touch to the album.

7.   Ordinary Fool (Paul Williams) 3:40
       Karen and Richard worked on this tune back in 1976 during the "A Kind of Hush" sessions. It is a mystery to many as to why the song was not included on the album. Evidently, the song is superior to others that made it, such as "Breaking up Is Hard to Do," "Goofus," "There's a Kind of Hush," even "Can't Smile Without You." Some fans feel had the song been released in 1976 it may have been a hit.

       In her own smooth and rich style Karen Carpenter gives you that sense or feeling of sipping on a glass of wine in a smoky, jazz club where the torch singer is standing right there in front of you, singing her heart out. It is very much the same aura you feel while listening to "This Masquerade." John Phillips brings the song home with an extraordinary, sax solo (every bit as effective as any sax solo by Bob Messenger). "Ordinary Fool" is a highlight, not only on "Voice of the Heart," but in the entire output of the Carpenters' catalog.

       "Ordinary Fool" was used as the B-side on the Brazilian single release of "Now."

This Paul Williams song was never a hit single for anybody, but like many of his non-hit songs, this one has been recorded by many artists and is fairly well-known. Williams wrote the song in 1975, and recorded and released it on his 1975 A&M album of the same name. Many Paul Williams fans call "Ordinary Fool" one of his best albums. Shortly after the release of Williams' 1975 album, the song "Ordinary Fool" came to the attention of the Carpenters, and they recorded the song for inclusion on their forthcoming album "A Kind of Hush," but the song remained unreleased (until 1983). Had Carpenters released the song in 1976 they would have been the first popular act to release it. As history has it, a 1920's-styled, sweet-soul version of the song was used in the 1976 movie "Bugsy Malone," a movie in which Paul Williams wrote and scored the soundtrack. After the success of the movie, several jazz/blues-style artists recorded the song, including a smoky rendition by Ella Fitzgerald in 1977 and an equally moving version by Mel Torme also in 1977. In recent years the song made a resurgence when it was recorded by jazz/soul singer Niki King in 2002, and then again in 2008 by jazz/blues singer Ray Brown, Jr.

- **Note from Rick Henry:** *This is absolutely my favorite song from "Voice of the Heart," and probably the only song from this album that I go back to time-and-time again. It's Karen's vocal and that smooth, silky saxophone that get to me.*

8.   Prime Time Love (Mary Unobsky / Danny Ironstone)
3:10

This is one of those often-overlooked Carpenters' tunes that really deserves a reassessment by fans and critics alike. The song is a classy and vibrant 80's soft-rock tune, which has all the trademark Carpenters sounds, including a nice saxophone solo and an irresistible hook.

Initially this song was recorded during the 1980-81 "Made in America" sessions, but did not make it on the album. Like many of their outtakes "Prime Time Love" is seemingly stronger than much of what ended up on "Made in America."

Songwriter Danny Ironstone wrote this song in 1978 with co-writer Mary Unobsky. The song was first recorded and released in 1980 by English singer-songwriter Jess Roden on his Island Records album "Stone Chaser." This is most likely where Richard Carpenter first heard the song. Carpenters' arrangement is very similar to that found on Roden's album. Before he made it big as a solo artist, Luther Vandross performed back-up vocals on Roden's version of "Prime Time Love." In 1973, Roden teamed up with ex-Doors members Robby Kreiger and John Densmore to form the group, The Butts Band. Roden sang lead vocals on the two albums they released in 1974 and 1975.

Danny Ironstone reached his pinnacle as a songwriter in the 80's. He co-wrote several popular songs including "Any Old Sunday" by Chaka Khan (1981) and "Sooner or Later" by Dusty Springfield (1982). He also co-wrote quite a few songs with Mary Unobsky, including "Survivor" by Rita Coolidge (1984) which was used as the B-side to her hit "Something Said Love." Ironstone and Unobsky also wrote "Don't Break My Heart" by Sheena Easton (1985) and "Crime of Passion" by Bonnie Raitt (1986).

Mary Unobsky has a long and successful resume as a songwriter. Her first hit to be recorded was "That Kind of Woman" which was done by Merilee Rush in 1968, and used as the B-side to the mega-hit "Angel of the Morning." Others to record songs co-written or written by Mary Unobsky include Florence Henderson (yep, Carol Brady), Rita Coolidge, Jackie DeShannon, Booker T. Jones, Sam Harris, Nancy Wilson and a host of others. As a matter of fact, Sam Harris recorded Mary's song "I've Heard It All Before" for his debut album which included several Carpenters regulars such as Tony Peluso (guitarist for Carpenters), Maxine Willard Waters and Julia Tillman Waters (both sang backing vocals on "Passage" and "Made in America") and

Paulinho DaCosta (who played percussion for Carpenters on a few of their albums).

- **Note from Rick Henry:** *I really enjoy this song quite a bit. I like the modern feel; I call it "cosmopolitan." This is my second favorite track from "Voice of the Heart."*

9.   <u>Your Baby Doesn't Love You Anymore (Larry Weiss)</u>
3:51

Another outtake from the "Made in America" sessions features yet another excellent vocal by Karen recorded in 1980. The song features a nice, bass line and some appealing brother and sister harmonies behind Karen's lead vocal. Some have suggested that in portions of the song Karen sings a tad bit too high for her comfort range. This may be true due to the fact that this is a "work lead" not intended for release. Had the song been chosen for inclusion on "Made in America," Karen would have gone back into the studio to rerecord her vocals and fine-tune the pitch, tone and key of her voice. As it is, this "work lead" is a superior performance by Karen.

The song was submitted to Carpenters in 1980 for consideration. Its 60's sort of sound caught Richard's attention. It made him think of songs such as "Hurting Each Other" and "Hurts So Bad." Carpenters recorded the rhythm track and Karen's work lead in 1980. Additional instruments and mixing were done in 1983 for inclusion on "Voice of the Heart."

"You're Baby Doesn't Love You Anymore" was the second single released from "Voice of the Heart," however, it did not chart with the exception of reaching #12 on the US Billboard Adult Contemporary chart.

Ruby and the Romantics originally recorded "Your Baby Doesn't Love You Anymore" in 1965 (this is the second Ruby and the Romantics song Carpenters recorded, the first was "Hurting Each Other"). Although this song did not hit the charts for Ruby and the Romantics, it did receive a fair amount of radio airplay and is remembered by fans of the genre from that time period.

Songwriter Larry Weiss has enjoyed an immense amount of success as a songwriter. He's written and co-written songs which have been recorded by Nat King Cole, Dionne Warwick, Paul Anka, Lenny Welch, Eric Burdon and the Animals, Freda Payne, Canned Heat, Leslie gore, Engelburt Humperdinck, Dusty Springfield, Lou Rawls, Donny Osmond, Bobby Sherman, Cissy Houston, Maureen McGovern, Carl Douglas and others. He is best remembered for the song "Rhinestone Cowboy" which was a #1 mega-hit for Glen Campbell in 1975.

10.   Look to Your Dreams (Richard Carpenter / John Bettis)
4:28

The birth of this gem dates back to 1974 when Karen asked Richard to write a song that would be a cross between a standard and a show tune. At that point Carpenter and Bettis wrote the song, but it wasn't until 1978 that they finally recorded it. It was recorded during the same time as "I Believe You" and other pop tunes while they were working on "Christmas Portrait." Richard never included it on any Carpenters albums because he felt it was not contemporary enough for release. Regardless, Karen never forgot the song. Apparently this was Agnes Carpenter's (Karen and Richard's mom) favorite song.

Peter Knight (who was working quite a bit with Carpenters in 1977/1978) composed the sweeping arrangement adding to the song's reflective quality. Fans have called the song inspirational and hail the lyric as one of the best written by John Bettis. *"Look to your dreams and tomorrow may be better for you and me."*

Carpenters superfan, Ned Nickerson, has mentioned in his video for the song, "At the conclusion of the song, the piano continues the melody, implying that though The Voice has been silenced, the music continues." Here's a

link to his video:
http://www.youtube.com/watch?v=7XSYl9plYM4

Karen sings the song with a rich and deep, delicate sentiment and a superb sense of timing. Her performance is evidence that she would have fit well singing in front of a 40's-style, show-tune big band.

"Look to Your Dreams" was used as the B-side to the 1983 single release of "Make Believe It's Your First Time" and again for the 1984 single release of "Now."

An Old Fashioned Christmas (click here to purchase)
Released: October 1984
Producer: Richard Carpenter
Arrangements: Richard Carpenter, Peter Knight, Billy May
Lead Vocals: Karen Carpenter, Richard Carpenter
Background Vocals: Karen Carpenter, Richard Carpenter, The OK Chorale directed by Dick Bolks, The English Chorale directed by Robert Howes
Piano: Richard Carpenter
Keyboards: Richard Carpenter, Pete Jolly
Drums: Ron Tutt, Barry Morgan
Electric Bass: Joe Osborn
Upright Bass: Pete Morgan
Tenor Sax: John Phillips
Harp: Gayle Levant, Skaila Kanga
Engineer: Roger Young, Ray Gerhardt, Robert De La Garza, Eric Tomlinson
Assistant Engineer: Alan Rouse
Mixing Engineer: Roger Young, John Richards
Mixing Assistant: Jim Cassell, Mike Hatcher, Clyde Kaplan, Dave Marquette
Recorded at A&M Recording Studios
Mixed at A&M Recording Studios, Capitol Recording Studios and The Village **Art Direction:** Chuck Beeson
Album Design: Rebecca Chamlee with Chuck Beeson
Illustration: Chuck Beeson
Photography: Harry Langdon
Chart Positions: 190 (US)
Certifications: Gold (US)
Singles: Santa Claus Is Coming to Town (1974), Little Altar Boy

Rick Henry's Rating: 7.0

"An Old Fashioned Christmas" is a posthumous compilation of Christmas tunes (both secular and spiritual), which were recorded during the "Christmas Portrait" sessions in 1977-78. Carpenters had such a good time with "Christmas Portrait" that they recorded way more than what could fit onto one album. Along with these previously unreleased tracks Richard recorded a few new songs, most prominently the song "An Old Fashioned Christmas" which was written by Carpenter and John Bettis. Due to the ongoing popularity of Carpenters Christmas music "An Old Fashioned Christmas" sold fairly well making #190 on Billboard's Top 200 and was eventually certified Gold.

The additional recording and new recordings were largely done at Abbey Road Studios in the UK, which was a thrill for Richard, having been a lifelong Beatles fan. Seven of the fourteen songs feature Karen's lead vocals. But it isn't until the fifth track, "(There's No Place Like) Home for the Holidays," that we finally hear her voice, and what a treat it is. Another highlight is the inclusion of the ballad version of "Santa Claus Is Coming to Town," which first surfaced in 1974 when it was released as a single.

After having been out of print for several years, "An Old Fashioned Christmas" was released in its entirety as part of the double-disc release "Christmas Collection" which also included the entire "Christmas Portrait" album. Both albums were digitally remastered for this collection released in 1996.

- **Note from Rick Henry:** *I will only be reviewing the highlights of this album. Some songs will only be listed.*

1. <u>It Came Upon a Midnight Clear (Edmund Hamilton Sears / Richard Storrs Willis)</u> :43
   The album begins with Richard Carpenter's lead vocal on this a cappella song. The song is reminiscent of "Invocation" and "Benediction" from the 1969 album "Offering" and finds Richard's voice overdubbed many times over to create a nice choral effect. This opener

sets the mood for another wonderful album full of festive and inspirational music of the season.

2. Overture 8:18
    This medley includes the following songs:
    "Happy Holiday" (Irving Berlin)
    "The First Noel" (Public Domain, Traditional Old English Carol)
    "March of the Toys" (Victor Herbert)
    "Little Jesus" (Public Domain, from the Oxford Book of Carols)
    "I Saw Mommy Kissing Santa Claus" (Thomas Conner)
    "O Little Town of Bethlehem" (Public Domain, L.H. Redner)
    "In Dulce Jubilo" (Public Domain, 14th Century German Melody, P. Brooks)
    "Gesu Bambino" (Pietra A. Yon)
    "Angels We Have Heard on High" (Public Domain, Traditional French Carol)

3. An Old Fashioned Christmas (Richard Carpenter / John Bettis) 2:34
    This song was written by Carpenter & Bettis in 1984 specifically for this album release. The song starts off with an orchestral intro that works into a delicate choir singing John Bettis' lyrics and features Richard Carpenter in a smooth, falsetto lead vocal.

    As always Carpenter and Bettis prove they still have that magic touch in writing a most effective tune. John Bettis' lyric reminisces of Christmases of years gone by, and how he misses being with friends and family. It's a somewhat melancholy lyric. But Richard Carpenter's heartfelt arrangement brings the song a texture of warmth, setting the atmosphere of Christmas joy.

4. O Holy Night (Adolphe Adam / John Sullivan Dwight) 3:31

5. (There's No Place Like) Home for the Holidays (Al Stillman / Robert Allen) 2:13

This warm and cozy upbeat tune is one of the most popular Christmas tunes recorded by Carpenters. The song has made it as high as #18 on Billboard's Holiday Airplay chart and is especially popular in Southern California, where Carpenters began their career in music in 1965.

Reminiscent of songs such as "Top of the World" and "Those Good Old Dreams," "(There's No Place Like) Home for the Holidays" has that hint of country flair, a style that Carpenters dabbled with as far back as 1970 with "Reason to Believe." Karen displays a glowing sense of joy and enthusiasm as she sings this tune. It's a very uplifting song.

Lyricist Al Stillman and composer Robert Allen have written several hits together including: "You Alone (Solo Tu)" (1953/1961) by Perry Como, "Moments to Remember" (1955) and "No, Not Much" (1956) both by the Four Lads and "Chances Are" (1957) and "It's Not for Me to Say" (1957) both by Johnny Mathis.

- **Note from Rick Henry:** *This is my favorite song from this album. Quite possibly my favorite Carpenters Christmas tune.*

6. Medley 3:43
   "Here Comes Santa Claus" (Gene Autry / Oakley Haldeman)
   "Frosty the Snowman" (Steve Nelson / Jack Rollins)
   "Rudolph the Red-Nosed Reindeer" (Johnny Marks)
   "Good King Wenceslas" (Public Domain, John Mason Neale)

7. Little Altar Boy (Howlett Peter Smith) 3:43
   "Little Altar Boy" is a cherished, fan favorite, probably the favorite on the album as far as the fans are concerned. Karen Carpenter delivers one of her finest vocal performances of her entire career. Her performance is introspective and inspiring. She sings with a sense of mournful sadness. Her voice reaches right into the soul of the listener and leaves a mark that

is not soon forgotten. Although Karen's delivery is delicate and tender, the impact is bold and lasting.

Richard Carpenter ranks this soul-searching tune as one of his all-time favorite vocals by Karen.

"Little Altar Boy" was the only single release from "An Old Fashioned Christmas" and featured "Do You Hear What I Hear" on the B-side. The single is extremely rare and can fetch a price tag of $100 and up.

Songwriter Howlett Peter Smith wrote the song in 1957, and was also recorded by Andy Williams, Jack Jones, Vic Dana and Glen Campbell, although Carpenters' rendition remains the best known. Other than the song "Little Altar Boy," Howlett Peter Smith's career was mostly fueled by writing jazz tunes which were recorded by artists such as Don Ho, Spanky Wilson, Don Ellis, The Cunninghams, Gene Diamond, Bud Shank and Agnetha Faltskog.

8. <u>Do You Hear What I Hear (Noel Regney / Gloria Shayne)</u> 2:52

This song was originally intended to be recorded as a solo lead vocal by Karen, but ended up being a shared lead vocal by both Karen and Richard. Richard sings the opening verse because during the recording of her vocals, Karen either misplaced her music sheet or was preoccupied and sang the opening line as, "Hmm, hmm night wind to the little lamb," instead of, "Said the night wind to the little lamb." Karen's vocal on this recording is a "work lead" and was recorded in one take. Had the song been completed at the time, Karen would have gone back to the studio to re-record her vocal. As it stands Karen's "work lead" is astonishing, and her performance is especially lilting.

Carpenters released the song as the B-side to the single "Little Altar Boy." They have been fans of the song since Bing Crosby recorded it in 1963.

Written in 1962 by husband and wife team, Noel Regney (lyricist) and Gloria Shayne (composer), the song was a plea for peace during the Cuban missile crisis. It was first recorded by the Harry Simone Chorale and became a big hit that Christmas season. The following year Bing Crosby recorded the song (just one month before President John F. Kennedy was assassinated). Crosby's version became a huge hit and has been issued on a countless amount of compilations. Hundreds of artists have recorded the song as diverse as: Andy Williams, Jim Nabors, Mahalia Jackson, Bob Dylan, Gladys Knight, Glen Campbell, Mannheim Steamroller, Rosie O'Donnell (with special guest Elmo), Celine Dion, Sufjan Stevens and a host of many others.

Noel Regney also wrote the English lyrics for The Singing Nun's famous song "Dominique," which became a worldwide hit reaching #1 in the US, #2 in Norway and #6 in the Netherlands. Regney and Shayne also wrote "Rain, Rain, Go Away," based on the nursery rhyme; Bobby Vinton took the song to US #12 in 1962. "Goodbye Cruel World" (another Regney and Shayne composition) was a hit in 1961 reaching US #3 and UK #28.

9.　My Favorite Things (Richard Rodgers / Oscar Hammerstein II) 3:54

10.　He Came Here for Me (Ron Nelson) 2:12
Another soul-searching classic much in the same vein as "Little Altar Boy," this song showcases Karen deep and rich vocal power. This is one of several, spiritual choral pieces recorded during the 1978 "Christmas Portrait" sessions. "Silent Night" and "Ave Maria" round out Carpenters' spiritual recordings.

Written in 1960 by composer Ron Nelson, this song was composed for a four-part choir featuring either soprano, alto, tenor and baritone or soprano, soprano, alto, alto. It is primarily written for a female choir or a mixed choir. Ron Nelson is a music academic having attained a bachelor's and master's degree in music, as well as earning a doctorate in composition. Dr. Nelson became a professor at Brown University in Providence, Rhode Island, in 1963, and remained there until he retired as Professor Emeritus in 1993. Dr. Nelson has composed both classical pieces and popular music. The bulk of his work lies within classical and choral works. "He Came Here for Me" is his best-known work, primarily due to Carpenters having recorded the song. Some of his other compositions include "Fanfare for Kennedy Center," "Rocky Point Holiday," "Savannah River Holiday," "Ring Out Wild Bells," "Pebble Beach Sojourn," "For Katharine in April," "Ask the Moon," "He's Gone Away," "Jehovah, Hear Our Prayer" and many others.

11. <u>Santa Claus Is Coming to Town (Haven Gillespie / John Frederick Coots)</u> 4:04
This is the original, slower-ballad version of the song, which Carpenters released in 1974, at the same time they released "Please Mr. Postman." Richard Carpenter took this song, which is generally recorded as a quick and fun upbeat number, and turned it into a torch song classic (much as he did with "Ticket to Ride"). Karen's vocal, as always, is crisp and clear with some fantastic, dubbed-backing vocals by Karen and Richard. Most thrilling of the song is the great sax solo that just transforms this song into a winter-fest of warm feelings for the season.

While recording "Christmas Portrait" in 1977-78, Carpenters did a more traditional, shorter recording of "Santa Claus Is Coming to Town" for the album, but it does not come close to the range and emotion evoked from this torch-song version.

J. Fred Coots and Haven Gillespie wrote "Santa Claus Is Coming To Town" in 1934. It was first performed on Eddie Cantor's radio show later in the year. Hundreds of artists have recorded the song including Bruce Springsteen, Mariah Carey, Beach Boys, Frank Sinatra, Paul Anka, Rod Stewart, Ella Fitzgerald, Ray Charles, Lena Horne, Bing Crosby, Michael Bolton, Tony Bennett, The Supremes, Glee, Smokey Robinson, Willie Nelson,

Colbie Caillat, Dolly Parton, Sufjan Stevens, Gene Autry, Rita Coolidge, James Taylor, Chicago, Barry Manilow, Justin Bieber, B2K and many, many others.

Songwriters J. Fred Coots and Haven Gillespie wrote a few other hits in the 1930's including "You Go to My Head" a hit for many artists including Teddy Wilson and Billie Holiday.

12.   What Are You Doing New Year's Eve? (Frank Loesser)
2:51

This fantastic tune showcases Karen Carpenter singing to a 40's-styled, big-band setting. This is a genre in which Karen Carpenter is especially suited. It's as if she was born to sing these types of songs, from an era before her time. She sings with a certain musical flair and movement giving the song a gesture of calm, joyful peace.

The British-born maestro Peter Knight composed the understated, yet lush musical arrangement for this song. As a reminder Knight first came to major prominence in 1967 when he composed the orchestration for the Moody Blues' classic album "Days of the Future Passed." In 1977, he began working with Carpenters. His Carpenters contributions included either orchestration or arrangements for the songs "Calling Occupants…," "Don't Cry for Me Argentina," "I Just Fall in Love Again," "Because We Are in Love (The Wedding Song)," "Look to Your Dreams" and several tunes from both "Christmas Portrait" and "An Old Fashioned Christmas".

"What Are You Doing New Year's Eve?" was written in 1947, and first charted for American R&B group the Orioles. Margaret Whiting was amongst the first to record the song. Since then the song has been recorded by countless musicians/singers.

Songwriter Frank Loesser is best known for writing the music and lyrics for the Broadway musicals "Guys and Dolls" and "How to Succeed in Business Without Really

Trying." Loesser also wrote "Baby It's Cold Outside" another seasonal favorite, which is played every year at Christmas. Loesser's works have won a variety of awards, including Academy, Pulitzer Prize, Grammy and Tony awards. A few other popular tunes he has written include "I Don't Want to Walk Without You" and "Inchworm."

- **Note from Rick Henry:** *I love the 40's big-band feel of this song. This rates amongst my favorite Carpenters tunes.*

Time (Richard Carpenter solo) (click here to purchase)
Released: October 11, 1987
Producer: Richard Carpenter
Arrangements: Richard Carpenter
Lead Vocals: Richard Carpenter, Dusty Springfield, Dionne Warwick, Scott Grimes
Background Vocals: Richard Carpenter, Scott Grimes
Drums: Paul Liem
Percussion: Paulinho DaCosta
Keyboards: Richard Carpenter
Lead Guitar: Tony Peluso
Electric Guitar: Tim May
Bass: Joe Osborn, Bill Lanphier
Tenor Sax: John Phillips
Alto Sax: John Phillips
Flugelhorn: Herb Alpert
Synthesizer: Jim Cox
Concertmaster: Jimmy Getzoff
Engineer: Robert Young
Assistant Engineer: Robert DeLaGarza, Michael Bowman, Rob Jacobs
Mastering Engineer: Arnie Acosta
Mix-down Engineer: Robert Young
Mix-down Assistant: Robert DeLaGarza, Michael Bowman, Rob Jacobs
Recorded at A&M Recording Studios
Mixed at A&M Recording Studios
Contractor: Jules Chaikin, Jimmy Getzoff
Art Direction: Chuck Beeson
Photography: Larry Williams

Special Thanks: Ron Gorow, Roger Young, Werner Wolfen, Mark Levy, Joe Gottfried, Richard's lovely wife Mary
Personal Management: Joe Gottfried, Carman Productions, Inc.
Chart Positions: None
Certifications: None
Singles: Something in Your Eyes, Who Do You Love, Time
Rick Henry's Rating: 7.0

"Time" is the first of Richard Carpenter's two solo albums. Richard Carpenter began working on the album in 1986 (three years after Karen passed away). It took him over a year to complete the album. Generally, Carpenters spent only three to four months recording an album, but Richard took his time on this one.

The album features three guest singers, Dusty Springfield, Dionne Warwick and Scott Grimes. Richard sings lead vocals on six of the ten songs and does backup vocals on all of them. The song "When Time Was All We Had" is a dedication to Karen Carpenter and contains a stunning performance on the flugelhorn by Herb Alpert. Richard Carpenter wrote or co-wrote six of the songs with two of them being written with longtime collaborator John Bettis.

1. Say Yeah (Paul Janz / Pamela Phillips Oland) 3:49
    This is one of those songs that I often find myself saying had Karen lived she would have sung the living daylights out of it. I could hear her singing it and making a huge hit with it.

    This upbeat, pop, dance song is very much in tune with the direction of popular music in 1987. The song includes some excellent guitar work, catchy percussion patterns and snappy synthesizer programming. Richard's lower voiced background vocals add a little muscle to the song. Definitely a tightly produced song.

    Songwriter Paul Janz was a popular Canadian contemporary Christian artist having recorded his own albums and making a few hits including "Every Little Tear," "Rocket to My Heart" and "Stand." Paul began his career in music with his brothers, Ken and Danny, in the Christian band Deliverance. They charted in the US in 1979 with the hit "Leaving LA." Paul Janz recorded three albums for A&M Records in the years from 1985 to 1990; this is most likely how Richard came to discover the song "Say Yeah." Janz's songs have been recorded by Shania Twain, Greg Rolie and Gloria Loring.

Pamela Phillips Oland has had a hugely successful career as a songwriter. She writes songs which cross the musical genres including pop, R&B, country, jazz, musicals and rock. Her songs have been recorded by artists such as Whitney Houston, Frank Sinatra, Brothers Johnson, Gladys Knight, The Spinners, Anne Murray, Jacksons, Isaac Hayes, Commodores, Peabo Bryson, Aretha Franklin, Selena and many others. She has had more than 500 songs recorded.

- **Note from Rick Henry:** *This is my favorite song from "Time." I really enjoy the upbeat groove and synthesized percussion work. I am always thrilled about the possibilities this song may have possessed had Karen lived and recorded it. I think it could have been a hit.*

2.   Who Do You Love (Mark Holden / Peter Hamilton / Gary Pickus) 3:14

This nice, pop tune includes an infectious, deep-harmony vocal done by Richard with some nice Beach Boys-like background voices.

"Who Do You Love?" was released as a single in 1987, and featured "When Time Was All We Had" on the B-side.

3.   Something in Your Eyes (featuring Dusty Springfield)(Richard Carpenter / Pamela Phillips Oland) 4:11

This is the so-called "hit single" from the album. It didn't chart anywhere except on the Billboard's US Adult Contemporary chart on which it reached #12. The song received a fair amount of adult contemporary radio play in 1987, largely due to Dusty Springfield. Had it been properly promoted the song most likely could have reached the Top 40 on the singles chart as well as charting in other countries around the world. As it is in 1987 Richard Carpenter was not an act high on radio programmers airplay lists.

"Something in Your Eyes" was originally slated for release as the first single to what would have been Carpenters' follow-up album to 1981's "Made in America." Unfortunately, Karen Carpenter passed away before she had the opportunity to record her vocals for the song.

Co-written by Richard Carpenter and Pamela Phillips Oland, "Something in Your Eyes" is one of three tunes from "Time" written by this duo. The other two songs they wrote are "When Time Was All We Had" and "That's What I Believe."

"Something in Your Eyes" has ended up on several Dusty Springfield compilations and has become a favorite of Dusty's many fans. Dusty's vocal performance on this song is as good as it gets. She proves she is one of pop music's finest. Although fans of Karen Carpenter have commented that although Dusty's vocal is excellent, it's just not Karen.

In 2008, Philippine singer Claire de la Fuente teamed up with Richard Carpenter to record the song "Something in Your Eyes." The song did well for Claire and revived her career. Claire is known as the Karen Carpenter of the Philippines and has had a long and successful career dating back to 1977.

4. <u>When Time Was All We Had (A Dedication to Karen) (Richard Carpenter / Pamela Phillips Oland)</u> 3:01
By all means this is an album highlight. Richard puts in a gentle and heartwarming lead vocal performance, but it is not Richard's lead vocal that makes this song a highlight. It's the dedication to Karen, the lyrics and the overall mood and emotion that make this song standout.

The song opens with one minute and forty seconds of Richard Carpenter singing an a cappella tribute to his sister Karen. As a lead vocalist Richard Carpenter is at best just okay, but he handles this song ably and manages to deliver the emotion and tone the song calls for. Like many other Carpenters songs, this one relies heavily on the overdubbed vocal style, which was a famous trademark of Carpenters music throughout their career. This time the overdubs are done with Richard's voice only and the effect is still fantastic.

"When Time Was All We Had" was used as the B-side to the 1987 single "Who Do You Love?"

In the lyric (written by Pamela Phillips Oland) *"I will never forget your face in silhouette"* brings to mind the famous Carpenters silhouette images that were used alongside their logo in advertisements and picture sleeves. The first silhouette image surfaced around late 1971 or early 1972. A new silhouette with Karen's hair parted in the middle first came about in 1975. Finally the ultimate silhouette was the cover of "Made in America." You can see an image of the 1972 silhouette at the following link: http://i127.photobucket.com/albums/p133/morepics03/carpenterssilhouette_zps1d35c8b7.png

The 1975 silhouette can be found at this link: http://i127.photobucket.com/albums/p133/morepics03/CarpentersOnlyYesterday_zps5ad37dbb.jpg

- **Note from Rick Henry:** *All-in-all, I really like this song. I am most touched by the lyrics, and Herb Alpert's flugelhorn is out-of-this world fantastic!*

5.   Time (Richard Carpenter) 3:32
"Time" is a tender piano instrumental which showcases Richard's delicate finesse with the instrument.

"Time" was used as the B-side to the 1987 single "Something in Your Eyes." In 1998, the song was released as an A-side single with "Calling Your Name Again" as the B-side.

6.   Calling Your Name Again (Richard Carpenter / Richard Marx) 4:15
Richard Marx is the singer/songwriter who had nine Top 10 hits in the US including the mega-hits "Endless Summer Nights" (1988) and "Right Here Waiting" (1989). Marx is a successful songwriter with his songs recorded by artists such as Kenny Rogers, Cliff Richards, Luther Vandross, N Sync, Sarah Brightman, Barbra Streisand, Natalie Cole, Josh Groban, Michael Bolton, Keith Urban, Celine Dion, Chris Daughtery and many others.

"Calling Your Name Again" was used as the B-side to the 1988 single "Time."

7.   In Love Alone (featuring Dionne Warwick) (Richard Carpenter / John Bettis) 3:15
Like "Something in Your Eyes," "In Love Alone" was written in 1982 expressly for Karen to sing on their follow-up album to "Made in America." Richard had planned on playing the song for Karen at a Christmas party he was hosting. It was raining heavily, and Karen decided she didn't want to drive the freeway that night. Sadly, she passed away less than two months later, so she never got to hear the song.

While recording the song for his solo album, Richard employed Dionne Warwick to sing the song. His choice of Dionne Warwick was appropriate as she played a big part in trying to help Karen with her illness. Dionne had visited Karen several times while she was in New York receiving treatment.

Dionne Warwick has expressed her gratitude in having the opportunity to record this lovely song, which was written especially for her friend to sing. Warwick has said this was one of the hardest things (emotionally) that she's ever done.

Because of the friendship and connection between Karen and Dionne, several fans have said they see this song as if Karen were singing and speaking through Dionne Warwick.

9.   Remind Me to Tell you (Mark Mueller)

10.   That's What I Believe (Richard Carpenter / Pamela Phillips Oland)
Scott Grimes performed the lead vocal for this song; he was 15 years old when he recorded it. Richard Carpenter produced Scott Grimes' eponymously-named debut album which was released in 1989.

11.   I'm Still Not over You (Richard Carpenter / John Bettis)

Lovelines (click here to purchase)
Released: October 31, 1989
Producer: Richard Carpenter / Phil Ramone
Arrangements: Richard Carpenter, Peter Knight, Rod Temperton, Bob James
Lead Vocals: Karen Carpenter
Background Vocals: Karen Carpenter, Richard Carpenter, The OK Chorale, Siedah Garrett,
Drums: Ron Tutt, John Robinson, Cubby O'Brien, Liberty Devitto
Percussion: Paulinho DaCosta, Ralph McDonald, Airto Moreira
Keyboards: Richard Carpenter, Greg Phillanganes, Pete Jolly, Bob James, Rob Mounsey
Guitars: Tony Peluso, Eric Johns-Rasmussen, David Williams, Tim May, David Brown, Russell Javors
Electric Guitar: Tony Peluso
Acoustic Guitar: Tim May
Steel Guitar: Jay Dee Maness
Bass: Joe Osborn, Louis Johnson, Doug Stegmeyer
Tenor Sax: Michael Brecker (If I Had You)
Oboe: Earl Dumler
English Horn: Earl Dumler
Flute: John Phillips (Slow Dance)
Harp: Gayle Levant

Engineer: Jim Boyer, Glenn Berger, James Guthrie, Ray Gerhardt, Roger Young,

Assistant Engineer: Bradshaw Leigh, Chaz Clifton, Dave Iveland, Ralph Osborn, Randy Pipes, David Crowther, Robert De La Garza

Mastered by: Mike Reese at A&M Mastering Studio

Mixing Engineer: Phil Ramone, Jim Boyer, Robert De La Garza

Mixing Assistant: Greg Goldman, Robert De La Garza

Recorded at A&M Recording Studios in Hollywood, CA, A&R Recording Studios in New York City, NY, Kendun Recorders in Burbank, CA

Art Direction: Chuck Beeson

Design: Peter Grant

Photography: Norman Seeff (front cover), Ed Caraeff (back cover)

Special Thanks: Greg Goldman, Roger Young, Robert De La Garza, Ray Gerhardt, Ron Gorow, Peter Knight, Karen Ichiuji, Roberta Kleine, Nancy Sorkow, David Alley, Billy Jones/Ardent Travel

Chart Positions: #73 UK

Certifications: None

Singles: Honolulu City Lights (1986), If I Had You (1989)

Rick Henry's Rating: 7.4

Released in 1989. "Lovelines" commemorates the 20th Anniversary of their first release on A&M Records. This collection includes twelve songs, ten of which were previously unreleased, four of them from Karen's solo recordings. The other eight songs were recorded between 1977 through 1980 and are a mix of outtakes from the TV Specials "Space Encounters" and "Music, Music, Music," and the albums "Passage," "Made in America," and songs recorded for an album that was to be released in 1978.

This is the first time the public has been treated to Karen's solo tracks. "Lovelines" has the honor of being the last Carpenters album/compilation to be released in the vinyl LP format. Richard Carpenter also announced that this would be the last Carpenters release of previously unreleased material.

Earlier in 1989, CBS Television aired The Karen Carpenter Story, a film chronicling the career of Carpenters. The film was a huge success and was the most watched program in the week it was aired. It was also the highest- rated television movie of the year and the third highest-rated television film of the entire decade. The film brought on a renewed appreciation and popularity of the Carpenters music.

Here is a listing of the recording dates of each song in this compilation; "Lovelines" (1980), "Where Do I Go from Here" (1978), "The Uninvited Guest" (1980), "If We Try" (1980), "When I Fall in Love" (1978), "Kiss Me the Way You Did Last Night" (1980), "Remember When Lovin' Took All Night" (1980), "You're the One" (1977), "Honolulu City Lights" (1978), "Slow Dance" (1978), "If I Had You" (1980), "Little Girl Blue" (1978).

1.   Lovelines (Rod Temperton) 4:28
       This compilation is named after and opens with this alluring song from Karen's solo recordings. Richard Carpenter obviously thought enough of the song to give it prominence on this collection.

       The version that shows up on this album was remixed by Richard Carpenter and is about 30 seconds shorter than the original on Karen's solo album. Richard took Karen's backing vocals and brought them to the front slightly, giving them more projection.

       To read the entire history of this song, please see the review I've written for Karen's solo album.

2.   Where Do I Go from Here (Parker McGee) 4:24
       This song was recorded in 1978 during the "Christmas Portrait" recording sessions and would have been included on the 1979 Carpenters album, which was never completed or released. One of the highlights (other than Karen's fantastic voice) is Tony Peluso's always awe-inspiring guitar solo, an integral part of Carpenters' music.

       "Where Do I Go from Here" was first recorded in 1977 by England Dan and John Ford Coley for their album

"Dowdy Ferry Road." Barry Manilow included it on his 1978 album "Even Now."

Songwriter Parker McGee achieved his first success when England Dan and John Ford Coley chanced upon "I'd Really Love to See You Tonight" a song written by the Mississippi native, Parker McGee. The song ended up topping the charts for England Dan and John Ford Coley in 1976. A few months later they had a second Top 10 hit with another Parker McGee written song "Nights Are Forever Without You."

Parker McGee's songs have been recorded by several artists including Gene Cotton, Jackie DeShannon, Tanya Tucker, Michael Johnson, Seals and Crofts, Pointer Sisters, Dan Hill, Crystal Gayle, George Harrison and others.

3. The Uninvited Guest (Buddy Kaye / Jeffrey M. Tweel)
4:24

This haunting, country-tinged, pop ballad was recorded in 1980 and was a top contender for placement on "Made in America" but didn't make it due to lack of space on the album. Karen sang this song with an aching tenderness in a way she had never sang before.

In the song's lyrics, Mary MacGregor's 1976, #1 hit "Torn Between Two Lovers" is mentioned. This is the only time a song title is mentioned in a Carpenters song.

On the cassette single release "The Uninvited Guest" was used as the B-side to "If I Had You."

Songwriter Buddy Kaye's biggest hit is 1949's #1 hit "'A' – You're Adorable (The Alphabet Song)," recorded by Perry Como with the Fontaine Sisters. He also co-wrote the theme song to "I Dream of Jeannie." Other songs written or co-written by Kaye include: "Speedy Gonzales" which was a hit for Pat Boone, "Mamacita" by Fats Waller and "The Old Songs" by Barry Manilow. Kaye wrote and co-wrote several songs for Elvis

Presley, including "(You're the) Devil in Disguise" and "Change of Habit."

Jeffrey M. Tweel is best known for having co-written the country music classic "Everytime Two Fools Collide" which was recorded by Billie Jo Spears in 1975 and became a huge hit for Kenny Rogers and Dottie West in 1978. Country artists such as The Kendalls and Billy Ray Cyrus have recorded his songs.

4.   <u>If We Try (Rod Temperton)</u> 3:42
"If We Try" is another Rod Temperton song from Karen's solo album. It was remixed again by Richard, but is not quite such an obvious mix as some of the other KC solo songs on this compilation. More details about this song can be found in the review of Karen's solo album.

5.   <u>When I Fall in Love (Edward Heyman / Victor Young)</u>
3:08

Originally, this song was written as an instrumental by Victor Young and was featured in the 1951 war film "One Minute to Zero." A few years later Edward Heyman added the lyrics, and it became a huge hit for Nat King Cole in 1957. Johnny Mathis, Etta James and The Lettermen have all charted with the song also.

Carpenters recorded this song in the same session with "Little Girl Blue" for their 1978 television special "Space Encounters." "Little Girl Blue" was chosen for that special, but "When I Fall in Love" was finally used in 1980 for their "Music, Music, Music" special. Famed British musician Peter Knight composed the sweeping arrangement for the song which was also included on the 1994 compilation "Interpretations," a 25th Anniversary Celebration of Carpenters music.

Songwriter Edward Herman wrote the lyrics for many hits including "You Oughta Be in Pictures," "For Sentimental Reasons," "Body and Soul," "The Wonder of You" and several others.

Conductor/Composer Victor Young conducted many of the famous big bands of the 40's including Jimmy Dorsey, Tommy Dorsey, Eddie Lang and many others. His compositions include "When I Fall in Love," "Moonlight Serenade," "Sweet Sue," "Love Letters" and many others.

6. <u>Kiss Me the Way You Did Last Night (Margaret Dorn / Lynda Lee Lawley)</u> 4:03
This is another of many outtakes from the 1980-81 "Made in America" sessions. The song was not released in 1981 due to the time and complexity it would take to mix the track down to a stereo version.

This is one of those few songs that contains vocals by someone other than Karen or Richard. Siedah Garrett joins Karen and Richard with the background vocals. Siedah is best remembered for singing a duet with Michael Jackson on the 1987 #1 hit "I Just Can't Stop Loving You." She also co-wrote Michael Jackson's #1 hit "Man in the Mirror."

Margaret Dorn's biggest claim to fame is co-writing "Kiss Me the Way You Did Last Night," which ultimately gained international prominence after it was released on Carpenters' "Lovelines" album in 1989. Lynda Lee Lawley co-wrote "How Could This Go Wrong," which became a semi-hit for Exile (Kiss Me All Over) in 1979.

7. <u>Remember When Lovin' Took All Night (John Farrar / Molly-Ann Leiken)</u> 3:47
This is another track from Karen's (still unreleased at the time) solo album. This all-out disco tune was co-written by John Farrar who is best known for writing and producing several hits (both songs and albums) for Olivia Newton-John from 1971 to 1989.

To read the entire history of this song please see the review I've written for Karen's solo album.

8. <u>You're the One (Steve Ferguson)</u> 4:13

Recorded in 1977 during the "Passage" sessions, it was a toss-up between "I Just Fall in Love Again" and "You're the One," as to which would make it on the album. Richard Carpenter said it was a flip of a coin that made the final decision.

Jennifer Warnes first recorded "You're the One" for her 1976 album "Jennifer Warnes," which also included the mega-hit "Right Time of the Night".

Songwriter Stephen Ferguson gained minor popularity as a songwriter in 1976, with his songs being recorded by artists such as Mary MacGregor ("Mama"), Andrew Gold ("Hope You Feel Good") and Jennifer Warnes (as mentioned above). Despite three popular artists recording his songs in 1976, it wasn't until 1989 (when Carpenters finally released "You're the One") that Ferguson achieved international acclaim.

Richard Carpenter has commented that he feels "You're the One" is one of Karen's finest vocals.

9.   Honolulu City Lights (Keola Beamer) 3:19
        Karen and Richard first heard this song in 1978 while on vacation in Hawaii and immediately fell in love with it. Once they got back home they recorded the song (during the same session with "Slow Dance") but never released it until 1986 when Richard released it as a single. The single received minor radio airplay but did not chart. Jay Dee Maness provides a fantastic, pedal steel guitar performance, which lends to the Carpenters' country-esque treatment of the song.

        Songwriter and guitarist, Keola Beamer, recorded the song with his brother, Kapono Beamer, and released it in early 1978. It was a huge hit in Hawaii and won several awards from the Hawaiian Music Industry.

10.   Slow Dance (Philip Margo / Mitchell Margo) 3:35
        Richard heard this song on the 1978 album by Kristy and Jimmy McNichol. He was somewhat unsure about recording the song due to the somewhat juvenile lyric,

but decided to record it anyway. Karen and Richard recorded the song in mid to late 1978 along with "Honolulu City Lights."

"Slow Dance" has several sibling ties to it. It was written by brothers Phil and Mitch Margo, and then first recorded by brother and sister act Kristy and Jimmy McNichol, and finally recorded by the ultimate brother-sister team Carpenters.

Brothers Mitch and Phil Margo started their careers in music at a very young age. Mitch, a multi-instrumentalist and first tenor was only 13 years old (in 1960) when he was recruited to join the vocal group The Tokens, while Phil, a baritone, was 18. The Tokens scored the #1 hit "The Lion Sleeps Tonight" in 1961; Mitch and Phil were well on their way to a super-successful career. As songwriters they wrote songs recorded by many popular artists such as The Tokens, Monkees, Chiffons, Astrud Gilberto and Tony Orlando & Dawn.

11.   If I Had You (Steve Dorff / Gary Harju / Larry Herbstritt) 3:57
This track is from Karen's solo album, which at this point in time (1989) was still unreleased. Richard Carpenter stated this was his favorite song from Karen's solo works.

Richard (as with the other KC solo songs on "Lovelines) remixed the song, most evidently the backing vocals. He did, however, replace Doug Stegmeyer's bass guitar and mixed in Joe Osborn on bass.

To read the entire history of this song please see the review I've written for Karen's solo album.

12.   Little Girl Blue (Richard Rodgers / Lorenz Hart) 3:24
Richard Carpenter chose to close this compilation with a song which poignantly suits Karen's voice to perfection. With her silky-smooth tones, Karen conveys

her emotions in this song almost as if the song had been written for her.

Lavishly arranged and orchestrated by Peter Knight, "Little Girl Blue" was recorded in 1978 and was featured in the Carpenters' ABC television special "Space Encounters."

Lyricist Lorenz Hart and composer Richard Rodgers were a successful Broadway songwriting team and wrote the music for 26 Broadway musical including "Jumbo" (1935), "On Your Toes" (1936) and "Pal Joey" (1940). Many of their hit musicals were during the Great Depression era of the 1930's. Some of their most notable songs include: "Bewitched, Bothered and Bewildered," "Blue Moon," "Little Girl Blue," "Mountain Greenery," "My Funny Valentine," and "The Lady Is a Tramp."

"Little Girl Blue" was written for the 1935 hit musical "Jumbo," which was about a financially struggling circus. In the musical, Gloria Grafton introduced the song. In 1943, Gloria Grafton dubbed Lucille Ball's singing in the musical "Best Foot Forward."

More than 50 singers including Louis Armstrong, Rosemary Clooney, Ella Fitzgerald, Judy Garand, Diana Krall, Linda Ronstadt, Diana Ross, Carly Simon and Frank Sinatra have recorded "Little Girl Blue."

From the Top (4-Disc Box Set) (CLICK HERE to purchase)
Released: 1991
Producer: Richard Carpenter
Compiled by Richard Carpenter

The four-disc, career-spanning box set was assembled and compiled by Richard Carpenter. It contains songs from the 1965 Richard Carpenter Trio sessions to "Now," the very last song Karen recorded in 1982.

I am only reviewing eight tracks from this collection as most of the tracks are previously released or are TV commercials. I am only reviewing the previously unreleased songs.

1. <u>Caravan (Irving Mills / Duke Ellington / Juan Tizol)</u> 3:37
    This instrumental showcases Carpenters' roots in (somewhat) abstract jazz. This is a musical style they would touch on throughout their career with songs such as "All I Can Do," "Another Song," "B'wana She No Home" and others. Recorded in 1965 under the name The Richard Carpenter Trio, Richard on keyboards was joined by his lovely sister, Karen, on drums and friend Wes Jacobs on bass and tuba. This is one of Richard Carpenter's earliest musical arrangements. Richard carefully arranged this song with the purpose of showcasing each musician in a solo spot, with a strong emphasis on Karen, who had only been playing drums for a few short months. The song was recorded live in the Carpenter family living room in Downey, California, during the hot weather of the summer in 1965. You can hear background chatter of friends and family members like giggles and other noises.

    "Caravan" is a jazz essential composed by Juan Tizol. Many recordings list Duke Ellington and Irving Mills in the songwriting credits. Ellington did not actually write this tune but his influence in this song is noted. Irving Mills wrote lyrics for the song and is often not credited in instrumental recordings. The first recording of "Caravan" was in 1936, an instrumental by Barney Bigard and his Jazzopators. All the band members in the Jazzopators were also members of Duke Ellington's Orchestra. Ellington played piano on the Barney Bigard recording.

    Puerto Rican trombonist and composer, Juan Tizol, also wrote the standard "Perdido." Tizol played in Duke Ellington's band from 1929 to 1944. After that he played with Harry James, Nelson Riddle and Nat King Cole. He made a brief return to Ellington's band in the early 1950's.

2. <u>The Parting of our Ways (Richard Carpenter)</u> 2:20

Recorded in 1966, this early Carpenters tune is rough around the edges but still displays a sense of budding musical talent. Hints of Karen's dark, velvety tones are barely heard but the potential is very much apparent. This song is one of the first songs recorded by Karen and Richard before Karen had been signed to Joe Osborn's Magic Lamp Records label. The original masters of this song were lost in a fire at the Osborn's home in 1975. All that was left of this song, which was recorded in Osborn's garage studio, was a worn, acetate disc.

3. Looking for Love (Richard Carpenter) 1:51
This was the first (and only) single released by Karen Carpenter on the Magic Lamp label. There were only 500 copies of the single (labeled ML 704) pressed. The record, which was recorded and released in 1966, is a highly sought after collector's item and is valued as high as $2,500 for a mint copy.

A somewhat determined and enthusiastic upbeat musical arrangement, which is finished by Karen's husky early vocals, envelops Richard Carpenter's dark lyric about an elusive love. It's an interesting tune showcasing the early talents of Karen and Richard on keyboards and drums, respectively, with assistance from Joe Osborn on bass.

4. I'll Be Yours (Richard Carpenter) 2:28
"I'll Be Yours" was used as the B-side of the 1966 Magic Lamp Records single "Looking for Love." Some people have commented that this should have been the A-side.

5. Iced Tea (Richard Carpenter) 2:36
This short, but sweet, instrumental is historical in the Carpenters' catalog of music for several reasons. This little, ambitious tune is an original written by Richard and performed by himself on piano and Karen on drums with friend Wes Jacobs on tuba. The piece is somewhat avant-garde and slightly experimental. Three quarters of the way into the song we are treated to a fantastic drum solo by the princess of drums, Karen Carpenter.

This tune holds up well to masterpieces by the likes of Dave Brubeck, Freddie Hubbard, Stan Getz and other greats.

"Iced Tea" paired with an instrumental performance of "The Girl from Ipanema" brought Carpenters their first brush with fame as the group, The Richard Carpenter Trio, when they performed both songs at the 1966 Hollywood Bowl Battle of the Bands. The trio won the competition. Neely Plumb, a west coast rep for RCA Records was in the audience and was taken by the trio. By September 1966, the group signed to RCA. In a minimum of time they recorded 11 songs for RCA, which were never released. RCA were not impressed with what they heard from the Carpenter trio. Other songs recorded at RCA include instrumental versions of "Every Little Thing" (Beatles) and "Strangers in the Night" (Frank Sinatra). Along with "Iced Tea," these are the only three songs from those RCA recordings to surface.

6.   You'll Love Me (Richard Carpenter) 2:27
With this song, recorded in 1967, Carpenters found themselves expanding their sound. Richard incorporated the electric piano, which gave the song a more contemporary sound. As the band headed into the late 60's musical styles were evolving and heading more toward an electric sound. The Beatles were spearheading this change in musical tastes.

Karen Carpenter again captured the attention of the music public by playing drums and singing lead vocals.

"You'll Love Me" discovered a refinement in the Carpenters overall sound and especially in Richard Carpenter's skills as an arranger. During this time period Richard developed an interest in constructing songs with multi-harmony vocals. This was the beginning of that famous, layered-vocal sound. Richard first became interested in this sound when he was singing in the choir at California State University at Long Beach. Choir director, Frank Pooler, introduced

Richard to John Bettis, and a great friendship (as well as professional partnership) developed. In this early song Bettis plays guitar and sings backing vocals but soon becomes the lyricist for many original Carpenters tunes. The band, known as the Summerchimes, also included Gary Sims (guitar and vocals) and Danny Woodhams (bass and vocals). Richard also met Gary and Danny from the Cal State University choir. Gary Sims and Danny Woodhams became part of the Carpenters touring band and remained with Karen and Richard to the very end. Gary and Danny also wrote the classic "Road Ode."

The Summerchimes got a deal on some recording time at a studio called United Audio, in Orange County, California. They recorded nine songs during these sessions. Recorded in May 1967, "You'll Love," is the only song from these sessions to have been released.

7. Canta/Sing (Joe Raposo) 3:20
    Due to requests from A&M affiliates in South America and Europe, the Spanish lyric was written and recorded a few months after the release of the original.

    The entire story behind the song "Sing" can be found in the entry for the album "Now & Then."

8. Good Friends Are for Keeps (Jon Silberman)
    This short ode to friendship is often referred to as the Bell Telephone Company theme song. Karen Carpenter's voice just really shines on this. It would have been nice to hear a full-length version by Carpenters. Glen Campbell actually recorded a full-length version of the song for inclusion on a various artists album released in 1975 called "100th Year Celebration Album – Good Friends Are for Keeps – America Sings of Telephones." The album was released to commemorate the 100th year of the telephone. "Good Friends Are for Keeps" was written specifically for this album. The shortened version was used for an ad campaign for the Bell Telephone Company. Several different artists recorded the shortened version for use in the ads.

The song was recorded in 1975 by a pared-down, Carpenters group comprising of Karen singing lead and backing vocals and playing drums. Richard sings backing vocals and plays keyboards. Tony Peluso plays bass guitar and electric guitar.

Songwriter Jon Silberman also wrote a semi-hit for UK pop band Guys n' Dolls called "Only Loving Does It," which reached UK #42 in 1978. "Good Friends Are for Keeps" is Siberman's best known work primarily due to Carpenters' inclusion of the song on this and also the Essential Collection box sets.

Interpretations: 25th Anniversary Celebration (CLICK HERE to purchase)
Released: February 7, 1995
Producer: Richard Carpenter
Compiled by Richard Carpenter
Chart Positions: #29 UK
Certifications: Gold (UK)
Singles: Tryin' to Get the Feeling Again (1994)

This compilation was released to commemorate the Carpenters' 25th year with A&M Records. Three of the songs on the album were previously unreleased, "Without a Song," "From This Moment On" and "Tryin' to Get the Feeling Again." The album was successful in the UK reaching #29.

I will only be reviewing the three unreleased songs.

1.   Without a Song (Vincent Youmans / Billy Rose / Edward Eliscu) 1:02
        Opening this compilation is an edited, short version of the song. To see the full review of this song please see below in the review for the 2001 album "As Time Goes By."

2.   From This Moment On (Cole Porter) 1:57
        This 1950 Cole Porter tune suits Karen Carpenter's voice just fine and conjures thoughts of how

magnificent a recording of the Cole Porter Songbook by Carpenters would have been. Carpenters recorded this song in early 1980 for their television special "Music, Music, Music," but it was not included in the show. Carpenters had been performing this song as early as 1976 when Ken and Mitzi Welch had been hired to revamp their stage show. A live version of the song shows up on the album "Live at the Palladium," which was released in November 1976.

"From This Moment On" was written in 1950 by Cole Porter for his musical "Out of This World," though the song never made it into the musical. It was, however, used in the 1953 musical film "Kiss Me Kate." Other notable recordings of the song have been done by Doris day (1950), Ella Fitzgerald (1956) and Frank Sinatra (1957).

Cole Porter has written many popular tunes including "Night and Day," "I Get a Kick out of You," "I've Got You Under My Skin," "Let's Do It, Let's Fall in Love," "Love for Sale," "Anything Goes," "It's De-Lovely," "In the Still of the Night," "Let's Misbehave," "Begin the Beguine," "So in Love," "Too Damn Hot" and several others.

- **Note From Rick Henry:** *It might be interesting to compile all the songs Carpenters recorded that were previously recorded by Sinatra. I'll have to look into that.*

3. Tryin' to Get the Feeling Again (David Pomeranz) 4:23
    Quite a few people regard this recording as a remake of a Barry Manilow tune, but in actuality Carpenters recorded the song before Manilow. Carpenters version was released 20 years after they recorded it, making it seem as if they may have recorded it after Manilow.

    Carpenters recorded "Tryin' to Get the Feeling Again" in January 1975, during the recording sessions for the album "Horizon." They decided not to include the song on the album because they felt there were already enough ballads on it. Over the course of time the song was misplaced and was thought to have been accidentally disposed. While working on a Carpenters karaoke album, in late 1991, engineer Roger Young found the song on a multi-track tape that contained "Only Yesterday." In 1994, strings and additional orchestration were recorded for inclusion on the compilation "Interpretations: A 25th Anniversary Celebration." Karen's vocal is a work lead that was recorded in a single take. Just before the two-minute mark you can hear Karen turning the page of her lyric sheet. For this reason alone Richard would have had Karen rerecord her near-perfect vocal performance. Karen Carpenter sings the song as it was originally written by David Pomeranz including the somewhat dark lyric, *"Like a bloodhound, searchin' for a long lost friend."* Manilow requested a rewrite of the lyric for his recording.

The song was released as a single in the UK where it reached #44 in 1994. This was Carpenters last chart single in the UK.

Both Gene Pitney and Lonnie Youngblood recorded "Tryin' to Get the Feeling Again" before Barry Manilow, but it was Carpenters who recorded it first. David Pomeranz wrote the song specifically for the Carpenters when he had heard they were looking for new songs to record for their upcoming album (Horizon).

Barry Manilow's recording was released as a single in early 1976 and reached #10 in the US.

Songwriter David Pomeranz is an ambassador for Operation Smile, which is a children's medical charity that provides cleft lip and palate surgeries for children worldwide. At the age of 19, Pomeranz was signed to MCA/Decca Records (as a singer) and recorded two albums with his second featuring Chick Corea. Pomeranz also wrote "The Old Songs," which was a Top 15 hit for Barry Manilow in 1981. Pomeranz's songs have been recorded by dozens of popular artists including Phoebe Snow, Kenny Rogers, Cliff Richard,

Sissy Spacek, Eddie Money, Engelburt Humperdinck, Cheryl Lynn, Bette Midler, Yvonne Elliman, Gene Pitney and several others. Pomeranz says he wrote, "Tryin' to Get the Feeling Again" during a time when he and his wife were going through some ups and downs.

- **Note from Rick Henry:** *Of all the songs released after Karen's death this is my particular favorite. It features one of Karen's strongest vocal performances and has that chill factor which was evident in many Carpenters tunes from the 70's. I also love this song because it was recorded during the sessions of my favorite Carpenters album, "Horizon." Awesome, just awesome!*

Karen Carpenter (solo) (click here to purchase)
Released: October 8, 1996
Producer: Phil Ramone
Arrangements: Rod Temperton, Bob James, Peter Cetera, Rob Mounsey
Orchestration: Bob James, Jerry Hey, Rob Mounsey
Lead Vocals: Karen Carpenter
Background Vocals: Karen Carpenter, Peter Cetera (harmony on "Making Love In The Afternoon)
Drums: Liberty Devitto, John "J.R." Robinson, Steve Gadd
Percussion: Ralph McDonald, Airto Moreira
Keyboards: Greg Phillanganes, Bob James, Rob Mounsey, Richard Tee
Guitars: Russel Javors, David Williams, David Bron, Eric Johns-Rasmussen
Bass: Louis Johnson, Doug Stegmeyer
Saxophone: Michael Brecker (If I Had You), Tim Cappello (Making Love In The Afternoon)
Engineer: Jim Boyer, Glenn Berger, James Guthrie, Ray Gerhardt
Assistant Engineer: Bradshaw Leigh, Chaz Clifton, Dave Iveland, Ralph Osborn, Randy Pipes, David Croather, Randy Pipe
Mastered by: Dave Collins, Ted Jensen
Mixing Engineer: Phil Ramone, Jim Boyer

Production Associates: Ed Sulzer, Michele Slagter, Laura Loncteau, Karen Ichiuji
Liner Notes: Phil Ramone, Richard Carpenter, Karen Carpenter
Recorded at A&M Recording Studios in Hollywood, CA, A&R Recording Studios in New York City, NY, Kendun Recorders in Burbank, CA
Art Direction: Chuck Beeson
Design: Rebecca Chamlee, Chuck Beeson
Photography: Claude Mougin
Photo Colorist: Amy Nagasawa
Conceptual Stylist: Paul Posnik
Fashion Coordinator: Phyllis Posnik
Hair Design: Joe Tubens C.H.D.
Make-up: Henriquez
Special Thanks: Roberta Kleine, Nancy Sorkow, David Alley, Billy Jones/Ardent Travel
Chart Positions:
Certifications:
Singles: If I Had You (1989), Make Believe It's Your First Time (1996)
Rick Henry's Rating: 9.7

The making of Karen Carpenter's solo album started out with a bit of confusion on Karen's part as she wanted to make sure she had Richard's blessing before she started the project. During the process of making the album she experienced much joy and excitement; it was the happiest time in her life. Yet the making of the album was a physically stressful undertaking for her. In the end her heart was broken when she was pressured to make the decision to shelve the album.

At the end of 1978, Richard left for Topeka, Kansas, to receive treatment for his addiction to Quaaludes. He spent most of 1979 at The Menninger Clinic. When he left Herb Alpert had suggested to Karen that it might be good for her to sink into a solo project. Karen took Alpert's advice. She hired Phil Ramone to produce the album, another suggestion from Alpert. Ramone, having been a fan of Karen Carpenter, was not interested in producing songs like "Sing" or "Yesterday Once More." He told her, "Your fans are no longer teen-agers. Why don't you grow up with them?" Olivia Newton-John had made the transformation from 70's sweetheart to "totally hot" 80's diva, and she was selling records in the multi-millions.

A&M Records subsidized $100,000 to make the album, while Karen put $400,000 of her own money into the project. Karen pulled no stops in producing the best album she could possibly produce. With Phil Ramone, she hired the finest musicians on the music scene and listened to songs submitted by the best songwriters at the time. Karen's solo project was an expensive undertaking. Once the album was completed Karen and Ramone sponsored a listening party in New York to very positive response. Then they took the album to Hollywood for a playback for Herb Alpert, Jerry Moss and Richard Carpenter. The response there was less than amicable. Herb Alpert liked the album; he just did not love it. Richard's response was the harshest. Karen's friend, Frenda Franklin, had commented that Richard didn't have to like the album, but he could have supported her in this venture. Franklin said to Karen this album wasn't just an album, it was her announcement of independence. The album meant a good deal to her. Karen had complete control over every aspect of the album, right down to the photo shots. With all her heart, Karen wanted to see the release of the album. But this was taken away from her as A&M executives and Richard Carpenter cajoled her into giving up the solo album to return to the Carpenters.

Producer Phil Ramone was one of the top producers at the time having worked with luminaries such as Paul Simon, Billy Joel, Barbra Streisand, Bob Dylan, Chicago, Elton John, Carly Simon, James Taylor, Frank Sinatra, Dionne Warwick, Stevie Wonder, Rod Stewart and a host of many others. Ramone's wife Karen Ichiuji developed a close friendship with Karen and remained her friend until her untimely death.

Musician extraordinaire, Bob James, orchestrated several of the songs on the album.

When Karen returned to Carpenters she recorded "Made in America," with Richard. They went in a slightly, newish direction, yet retained the basic Carpenters sound and philosophy. It was a complete, opposite direction of where Karen's solo album went. "Made in America" flopped, both critically and commercially. To this day it remains Carpenters' least selling studio album.

During this time not only did Karen experience the shelving of her beloved solo album and the failure of the Carpenters reunion album, but also entered into a marriage that was rocky from day one. Intertwined with all this her health was plummeting as she lost more weight and struggled with an eating disorder which she tried to hide from her friends and family. This was a very tumultuous time in Karen's life. It's as if she had a black cloud over her. In it all, she retained that golden voice that sounded great no matter what she sang.

Songs from Karen's album first appeared in 1989 on the posthumously released album "Lovelines." The album contained the songs "Lovelines," "If We Try," "Remember When Lovin' Took All Night" and "If I Had You." Two years later "My Body Keeps Changing My Mind" showed up in the box set "From the Top." Finally, after years of speculation and demands from fans, Karen's solo album was released in 1996, sixteen years after its completion, and thirteen years after her passing. Fans are torn over their response to the album. Some side with Richard's opinion and call it Karen Carpenter's worst work, while others find it to be an amazing and intricate album. As the years have gone by more and more fans are discovering that they actually do like the album regardless of the viewpoints of Alpert, Moss and Richard Carpenter. There are many out there including Olivia Newton-John, Quincy Jones and Phil Ramone (recently deceased) who have maintained their positive view on the album.

For more insights into the album take a look at the Karen Carpenter Avenue blog post, Behind The Music: Karen Carpenter Solo @ http://karenannecarpenter.blogspot.com/2013/04/behind-music-karen-carpenter-solo.html

- **Note from Rick Henry:** *I adore this album. It is a treasure in my record collection. When I first bought the album I put the headphones on and listened to the intricacies of the music and quickly recognized the layers of music so fantastically arranged. I was* *overtaken by Karen's vocal performance on these songs. It was a new Karen; she was exploring new territory with her voice, and in my mind was 100% successful in its execution. No, the songs do not feature the deep, dark, honey-blessed vocals that you hear on songs like "Superstar" or "Solitaire," and that is okay. Not every song she records has to display Karen as that "little girl blue." These songs showcase the upbeat side of Karen, that "girls just want to have fun" side. I rate this album within my Top Three favorite works of all albums done by Carpenters/Karen/Richard.*

1. <u>Lovelines (Rod Temperton)</u> 5:06
    The opening song "Lovelines" finds Karen Carpenter in great shape musically and vocally. In her first lines her voice is silky smooth, rich and deep; then she soars into a kaleidoscope of vocal range and electronically-treated backing vocals. The rhythm is upbeat with inflections of sunshine and good times. This is one of those upbeat tunes that makes you feel good. It's a great way to open the album.

    A great piano solo by Greg Phillinganes and some funky, bass work by Louis Johnson highlight the song. Phillinganes is a renowned keyboardist having worked with many top artists including Stevie Wonder, Quincy Jones, Donald Fagen, Lionel Richie, Eric Clapton and all of Michael Jackson's albums from 1979 onward. Bassist Louis Johnson developed a special friendship with Karen while working on her album. He admits he had a crush on her back in 1980, but at that point in time mixed-race relationships were considered taboo. Louis Johnson formed the popular A&M Records funk band Brothers Johnson with his brother George. They made hits such as "I'll Be Good to You" (1976), "Strawberry Letter 23" (1977) and "Stomp!" (1980). Johnson was also a successful, session player having played on albums by Michael Jackson ("Off the Wall," "Thriller," "Dangerous"), George Benson ("Give Me the Night"), Herb Alpert ("Rise") and several other top-notch jazz and funk albums.

"Lovelines" was written by one of the music businesses most underrated geniuses, Rod Temperton. Music was inbred for Rod Temperton as his father used to put a small radio in his crib at night instead of telling him bedtime stories. He first started out playing drums, and then went on to keyboards and other instruments (all of which he mastered). Temperton has had a hugely successful career in music. He first reached acclaim when he joined the disco/funk band Heatwave in 1974. He wrote and composed all the songs on their debut album, which included the mega-hits "Boogie Nights" and "Always and Forever." After that, he wrote and composed most of the songs on the next four Heatwave albums including the huge hit "The Groove Line." Beyond his success with Heatwave, Temperton's greatest successes came as a composer, songwriter, arranger and producer. He wrote the Michael Jackson tunes, "Rock With You," "Off the Wall," "Burn This Disco Out," "Thriller," "Baby Be Mine" and "The Lady in My Life." Temperton has also written or co-written, "Yah Mo Be There" which was recorded by James Ingram, "Masterjam" by Rufus, "Stomp" by the Brother's Johnson, "Love Is in Control" by Donna Summer, "The Dude" and "Razzamatazz" by Quincy Jones, "The Spice of Life" by Manhattan Transfer, "Love X Love" and "Give Me the Night" by George Benson, and many, many more hits.

Rod Temperton actually wrote "Off the Wall" and "Rock With You" specifically for Karen to record for her solo album. She turned down those two songs but did record three others, two of which made it on the album.

2.   All Because of You (Russell Javors) 3:31
       After hearing the eye-opening lush yet understated disco- thumping of "Lovelines" the album takes a turn into a completely different direction into an area Karen is more familiar, yet with a certain, raw soul not found on any Carpenters songs. "All Because of You," written by Billy Joel band mate Russell Javors, is a down tempo country-tinged tune which lets Karen express her

emotions without getting to overly sweet or confectionary. She puts as much of her soul into this song as any song she's ever done, although it's a different feel. There's more Karen upfront minus the multitude of backing vocals that sometimes get in the way of the purity of her voice. Here we are able to enjoy Karen Carpenter front and center.

Guitarist/songwriter/producer Russell Javors was thrilled when Karen had decided to record his songs. She recorded three in total: "All Because of You," "Still in Love With You" and the unreleased "Truly You." In Javors' original demo of "All Because of You" he opens the song with a slide guitar part. In Karen's rendition she hums the part where Javors played the slide guitar to great effect.

Russell Javors is best known as the primary guitarist in Billy Joel's backing band from 1976 to 1989. Other Billy Joel band mates joined Russell to record Karen's album include drummer Liberty DeVitto and bass player Doug Stegmeyer. Percussionist Ralph McDonald also played on several of Billy Joel's albums.

3.   If I Had You (Stephen Dorff, Gary Harju, Larry Herbstritt) 3:54

"If I Had you" is the album's most popular track having been released as a single in 1989 (from the "Lovelines" album). It reached #18 on the US adult contemporary chart. It enjoyed a fair amount of radio airplay and positive comments from music critics.

Many fans consider this song to be the album's strongest track with its funktified rhythms and Karen's soulful rendering. Richard Carpenter has also commented that this is his favorite track from Karen's album. Superfan Chris Tassin produced a fantastic music video for the song, which has received nearly half a million hits. Here's the link to the video:
http://www.youtube.com/watch?v=17tvW-5Uy7g

"If I Had You" began as a lyric written by Gary Harju (Harju has also written "Fire in the Morning" by Melissa Manchester, "Never Givin' up on You" by Johnny Mathis, "Maybe It's Time" by Marsha Hines and others). Gary Harju than took the completed lyric to Stephen Dorff and Larry Herbstritt (who often worked together); Herbstritt and Dorff. Larry Herbstritt took the chorus and Steve Dorff took the verse, and piece-by-piece they created "If I had You." When they wrote the song they didn't have any particular artist in mind; they just wrote what they felt. Larry Herbstritt's original vision for the song was to write a heavy metal chorus. Karen Carpenter was nowhere in his thoughts while he was writing the song. He was quite surprised when he heard she wanted to record the song for her solo album with Phil Ramone. Herbstritt was very happy with the song when he heard the completed recording. He felt Rod Temperton's vocal arrangement was more than exceptional.

Stephen Dorff is a prolific songwriter with too many songs to his credit to list. A few of his hits include "Ride 'Em Cowboy" by Paul Davis, "Takin' What I Can Get" by Brenda Lee, "You Set My Dreams to Music" by John Travolta, "Every Which Way but Loose" by Eddie Rabbitt, "Through the Years" by Kenny Rogers, "Only Love" by Wynonna, "Higher Ground" by Barbra Streisand and others.

Larry Herbstritt and Stephen Dorff also collaborated with Gary Harju on Melissa Manchester's "Fire in the Morning." The trio also wrote "Cowboys and Clowns" for Ronnie Milsap. Herbstritt and Dorff (along with two other co-writers) wrote the classic "I Just Fall in Love Again" featured on Carpenters' 1977 album "Passage." The duo also wrote Dionne Warwicke's "Easy Love."

Jazz saxophonist Michael Brecker provides the sultry saxophone solo in this song. Brecker is a hugely popular musician having won 15 Grammy awards. He's recorded about 30 albums as a solo artist with his brother and various groups he's formed. He's also been a sideman for many popular musicians including Aerosmith, Patti Austin, Average White Band, George Benson, Blue Oyster Cult, James Brown, Dave Brubeck, Eric Clapton, Chick Corea, Dire Straits, Donald Fagen, Jane Fonda, Aretha Franklin, Michael Franks, Art Garfunkel, Herbie Hancock, Bob James, Billy Joel, Chaka Khan, Manhattan Transfer, Dave Matthews, Charles Mingus, Willie Nelson, Laura Nyro, Yoko Ono, Jaco Pastorius, Esther Phillips, Lou reed, David Sanborn, Carly Simon, Paul Simon, Spyro Gyra, Ringo Starr, James Taylor, Lenny White, Frank Zappa and many, many more.

- **Note from Rick Henry:** *This song just blows my mind. I especially like Rod Temperton's vocal arrangement at the end with Karen's vocals multi-tracked and weaving in and out of each other to create a great, Manhattan Transfer sort of effect. I am certain had this been released as a single in 1980 it would have soared to the Top Five.*

4.   Making Love in the Afternoon (Peter Cetera) 3:57
This is one of the very few songs in Karen's entire career (after signing with A&M) where she sings with singers other than herself or Richard. The song features a silky lead vocal by Karen with a complementing harmony vocal by Peter Cetera. We all know Cetera for his work with the classic rock band Chicago. He was with the band from 1967 to 1985 and was one of the band's more popular lead vocalists. He also went on to a successful solo career achieving three Top Five hits and one Platinum album.

At the time Karen's album would have been released Chicago front man, Peter Cetera, was working on his first solo album, which was simply titled "Peter Cetera." Jim Boyer, who also did engineer work on Karen's album, produced Cetera's album. Longtime Carpenters associate, Tommy Morgan, played harmonica on Cetera's album. Amongst Carpenters fans Tommy Morgan is best remembered for his harmonica work on "Rainy Days and Mondays" and "Desperado." He's also featured on songs included on the albums "Made in America" and "As Time Goes By."

Producer, Phil Ramone had just completed work with Peter Cetera and Chicago producing the album "Chicago 13." While working with Chicago, Cetera had mentioned to Ramone that he was a big fan of Karen's voice. Cetera quickly went to work and wrote the song "Making Love in the Afternoon" expressly for Karen. Ramone and Karen invited Cetera to sing back-up on the song and billed it as a duet. Cetera also composed the arrangement of the song.

Fans of Karen's solo album call "Making Love in the Afternoon" infectious and consider it to be one of the album's best songs and strong enough to have been a hit single. Karen perfectly captures that lazy, California sunny afternoon feel with her natural silky tones.

- **Note from Rick Henry:** *Upon first listen of this album this song was immediately my favorite track. I thought to myself, this would have been an instant hit. Such a catchy, fun-loving song.*

5. <u>If We Try (Rod Temperton)</u> 3:46
    This smooth groove was written by Rod Temperton. Temperton was a master at writing soulful ballads with bits of light jazz infused. "If We Try" is one amongst many written by Temperton. Some of his other ballad compositions include; "The Lady in My Life" by Michael Jackson, "All About Heaven" by Brothers Johnson, "Mystery" by Manhattan Transfer and the classics "Baby Come to Me" by Patti Austin & James Ingram and "Always and Forever" by Heatwave. Each of these songs, if you listen to them, contains similar elements to what you hear in "If We Try."

    Rod Temperton put a good amount of work into Karen's solo album. In this particular song he not only wrote it but also composed the vocal and rhythm arrangements. Rob Mounsey (writer of "Guess I Just Lost My Head") did the song's orchestration. Louis Johnson (from the

A&M sibling duo Brother's Johnson) played a smooth mellow bass in the song. Louis Johnson was involved with quite a few of Rod Temperton's works. Louis Johnson compared Karen to Bjork in saying that Karen had the same sort of inner sadness as Bjork.

6. Remember When Lovin' Took All Night (John Farrar, Molly-Ann Leiken) 3:50
This all-out disco tune includes some jazz-fusion inflections and funk rhythms. The luminary Bob James arranged and orchestrated the song as well as performing the ethereal keyboard solo. Take a listen to Bob James' tune "The Walkman" from his 1980 album "H" and you can hear the similarities in his keyboard style.

Drummer, Liberty DeVitto, (from Billy Joel's backing band) says this is his favorite track from the album. He said, "It's the way everything fits together, the groove, her voice, the amazing background vocals. It's all there." DeVitto said the solo album was very important to her; she was ready to move on and get away from that cutesy, apple-pie image. DeVitto also commented that Karen was a perfectionist in the recording studio; while recording the background vocals for "Remember When Lovin' Took All Night" she put so much energy and effort into it that she ended up hyperventilating and passing out. DeVitto enjoyed working on Karen's album so much that he ended up falling in love with her. This seemed to be a common occurrence with the guys who performed on Karen's solo album, as bass player Louis Johnson also developed a crush on Karen during this time. What can we say? Karen is magnetic.

The song was co-written by John Farrar, who is best known for writing and producing several hits for Karen's friend Olivia Newton-John. Farrar was also a co-producer of the soundtrack for the 1978 movie "Grease" and he wrote the songs, "You're the One That I Want" and "Hopelessly Devoted to You."

Molly-Ann Leiken, who co-wrote the song with John Farrar, has co-written many tunes which have been recorded by a variation of artists such as Cilla Black, Greg Lake, Jane Olivor, Billie Jo Spears, Marlena Shaw, Barbara Fairchild, Yvonne Elliman, Tina Turner, Frankie Valli and others. Her best known song is "You Set My Dreams to Music," which was co-written by Stephen Dorff, who also co-wrote "I Just Fall in Love Again" and "If I Had You." John Travolta, Anne Murray, Dusty Springfield, Claudine Longet and Flower have all recorded renditions of "You Set My Dreams to Music."

- **Note from Rick Henry:** *As with many of the songs on Karen's solo album, I find the lead and backing vocals on this track to be especially engaging. Of course, master musician, Rod Temperton, contributed the exquisite, vocal arrangement.*

7. <u>Still in Love With You (Russell Javors)</u> 3:15
Upon first listen this song is an unexpected surprise. Some die-hard fans of the early Carpenters sound have written this one off as one of Karen Carpenter's worst recordings. There are also fans, willing to give Karen's new sound a chance, who hear and enjoy the song exactly for what it is. "Still in Love With You" is not meant to be a thought- provoking, mournful tune, as we grew accustomed to hearing from Karen most prominently in 1971 and 1972. "Still in Love With You" is a good-time song, one of those songs meant to elicit a smile on your face and put a groove in your step. Some detractors of the song have gone so far as to say that Karen is moaning and groaning in the song, although in reality she is rhythmically humming her parts throughout. There is no moaning or groaning in this song anywhere. Case in point, listen to Donna Summer's "Love to Love You Baby" if you want to hear moaning in a song.

"Still in Love With You" brings Karen Carpenter into the 80's with an infectious, new-wave beat, intoxicating percussive rhythms and energized guitar chords. Phil Ramone presents a Karen Carpenter we never knew existed; a thrill-filled Karen Carpenter. It's as if you can hear a smile in her voice as you listen to this song. No longer is she that "little girl blue," and she is happy to have escaped from that prison of perfection.

The song is credited as being arranged by Le' Band. Le' Band is actually Billy Joel's backing band comprising of Russell Javors, Liberty DeVitto, Doug Stegmeyer and David Brown; they all had a hand in piecing this song together. Javors commented that, "Phil wanted us to treat Karen like one of the guys. We had played together for so long, we were like a family. We were very comfortable working with each other. Phil Ramone wanted Karen to feel a part of what would surely be a different working environment than she was used to, not just a voice over a track. I guess we were a little wild in those days. We certainly didn't hold back in front of Karen. I really had the feeling that she was enjoying herself with us."

It was important to producer, Ramone, that Karen was involved in every aspect of the creation of this album. He didn't just want her to be the singer that came into the studio and sang her parts to the already recorded tracks. This project was to be Karen Carpenter's project.

Russell Javors has said that the song was not an easy one for Karen to sing; it was an attitude she had never explored before in song. He had the feeling that this was not an easy song for her to sing. Phil Ramone asked Karen to try singing the word "love" differently. Javors, says, "At one point I was actually in the vocal booth with Karen, and I lip-synched the lyrics while she was recording her vocal because she wanted to copy my phrasing. I was impressed at how hard she worked to put her stamp on it. Also, I was surprised at how softly she sang. Karen's voice was so rich and textured. Her voice was powerful without having to belt it out."

The New York Times had an article on the album when it was finally released. There was a mention that Agnes (mom) Carpenter wasn't happy hearing her daughter singing lines like *"I remember the first time I laid more than eyes on you."* Russell Javors thought it was cool that her mom remembered his song.

8. <u>My Body Keeps Changing My Mind (Leslie Pearl)</u> 3:46
This all-out disco tune is a favorite amongst Carpenters and first showed up on the box-set "From the Top" in 1991. When Karen began work on her solo album, producer Phil Ramone asked her what she wanted to explore. Karen answered that she loved Donna Summer. Karen did disco even though her brother, Richard, advised against it. Some call this Karen's revenge and feel this anthem could have been a dance floor hit in 1980.

Songwriter Leslie Pearl wrote the hits "Girls Can Get It" (1980) which was recorded by Dr. Hook and "You never Gave Up On Me (1984) recorded by Crystal Gayle. Karen Kamon (aka Karen Ichiuji or Karen Ramone) recorded the Leslie Pearl tune "You Can Do Better Than That" for her 1984 album "Loverboy." Of course, Karen Kamon is Phil Ramone's wife and also one of Karen Carpenter's best friends. Leslie Pearl had a hit of her own "If the Love Fits" which reached #29 on the Billboard singles chart in 1982.

9. <u>Make Believe It's Your First Time (Bob Morrison, Johnny Wilson)</u> 3:12
For further information on this song see the review from the "Voice of the Heart" album.

Karen's voice is up front and center on this song without the build-up of backing vocals or harmonies. Karen's singular voice transcends as mesmerizing warmth of hopeful yearning. Bob James' gentle piano work builds up into a gentle burst of sound which never becomes to overpowering. It's the perfect blend of intimacy and strength.

The song was released as a CD single in Japan in 1996 and has become a rare collectible.

It seems that overall, fans of Carpenters/Karen Carpenter prefer this more simple and toned down, intimate reading of this song as compared to the version which shows up on the posthumously released "Voice of the Heart" album. Many say the VOTH version is over-produced.

Karen first recorded this song in 1979 for her solo album. After it had been decided to shelve the album Richard Carpenter decided to re-record the song for the album "Made in America." In the end the song didn't make it onto MIA but was finally released two years later on the album "Voice of the Heart."

Several fans have felt that Karen's solo rendition of the song could have been a hit single in 1980 and consider it to be one of her best and most intimate vocal performances.

- **Note from Rick Henry:** *Simply put, I love this song.*

10. <u>Guess I Just Lost My Head (Rob Mounsey)</u> 3:36
With this song we are exposed to the flirty side of Karen Carpenter. This is a side of her personality we had never seen before; the fun and flirty, cute girl next door. It's a style that suits Karen well.

This lite jazz tune could have fit well on the radio alongside songs such as Captain and Tennille's "Do That to Me One More Time" and Barbra Streisand's "Guilty." This one is a natural for a single release with its catchy hooks and up-tempo rhythms.

Rob Mounsey wrote, orchestrated and arranged "Guess I Just Lost My Head." His delightful keyboard solo is a highlight of the song. Rob Mounsey has had a long career in music having worked with almost anybody you can think of in the music industry. His resume reads like a Who's Who in the music business. His most recent credits include Mary J. Blige, Usher, Deborah Cox, Rihanna and others. His strings mix of "Maybe Tomorrow" will be featured on the upcoming release

"Michael Jackson Remix Suite III." He's also worked with Steely Dan on their "Gaucho" album, Paul Simon's "Graceland," Madonna's "Crazy for You," Phil Collins' "Against All Odds" and several Michael Franks albums.

Written by Rob Mounsey, November 2004, NYC:

I was invited to work on Karen's project by Phil Ramone, someone I've worked with for many years (and as recently as last month). I was very young and new to the NYC recording scene.
Karen was very smart, very gifted and accomplished, and very nice. She gave me what may have been her greatest compliment – She likened me to her brother Richard. Many of the band members were members of Billy Joel's band – my pal, David Brown from Boston, Russell Javors, Doug Stegmeyer, Liberty DeVitto, etc. It was funny that the frequent, four-letter-words from the musicians upset her. She told us that she really didn't like to hear the "F" word. She really was kind of a "good girl" – very typical of an anorexia sufferer – but she had a sense of humor about herself.

I was so happy that she wanted to do my song ("Guess I Just Lost My Head"). The only problem was that it was really a man's song to sing to a woman. The second line was *"I was only watching the flower in your hair..."* Not being a congenital lyricist I was stumped for a substitute line, and it was Karen who came up with *"Only trying to memorize you there,"* which I thought was okay, and probably the best thing we would come up with.

It was no secret that her brother Richard really didn't like the record. For one thing, he thought that Karen should always sing in her trademark, basement register.

I was so shocked and sad to hear of Karen's death shortly thereafter. She was really a great, great person and a major talent.

- **Note From Rick Henry:** *"Guess I Just Lost My Head"*
  is my favorite song from the album. I'm not quite sure
  what makes it my favorite... could be the easy-going,
  laid-back flirty fun of it all.

11. <u>Still Crazy After All These Years (Paul Simon)</u> 4:17
    As in familiar Carpenters tradition, Karen Carpenter
    took this already familiar song and made it her own.
    Whereas Paul Simon's rendition was in a
    straightforward, classic, pop style, Karen adorned the
    song with a classy, brass section, some funky bass
    rhythms and an overall mellow, jazz feel. She turned a
    hot song into a cool tune.

    Rob Mounsey ("Guess I Just Lost My Head") arranged
    and orchestrated the tune and added his capable,
    keyboard parts and a sleek, guitar solo by David Brown
    from Billy Joel's live band.

    Paul Simon originally recorded this song in 1975, and
    included it on his album of the same name. The song
    was a popular, album track and was released as the
    album's third single after the #1 hit "50 Ways to Leave
    Your Lover." Paul Simon put "I Do It for Your Love" on
    the B-side of "Still Crazy After All These Years." Karen
    also recorded "I Do It for Your Love" but it has remained
    unreleased. However, it was leaked to the Internet
    along with eight other unreleased songs in the late
    1990's.

12. <u>Last One Singin' the Blues (Peter McCann)</u> 3:29
    Karen isn't discovering any new territory with this song.
    However, she does sing it in a lazy, sort of bluesy, jazz
    vocal, which we're not accustomed to hearing from her.
    Probably the closest she got to this sort of vocal in a
    Carpenters song is with "Ordinary Fool." This sort of
    lazy, smoky vocal is quite appealing for Karen.

    The song is an outtake not meant to have been on the
    album. A small bit of tweaking was done in order to
    include it as a bonus track when the album was released
    in 1996. In the beginning of the song you hear some

finger snapping, and Karen saying the words "Just a zinch slower, Lib." She was speaking to drummer Liberty DeVitto, who was cuing up the rhythm for the song. This opening paved the way for one fantastic tune. Somewhere around 2:40 she also speaks a few words, saying, "Don't forget the break."

"Last One Singin' the Blues", despite it being an outtake, is a fan favorite.

The song was written by singer/songwriter Peter McCann, who first reached fame in 1977, when Jennifer Warnes took a song he wrote, "Right Time of the Night," into the Top 10 in both the US and Canada. A few months later he had his own Top 10 hit with "Do You Wanna Make Love." McCann also wrote "Midnight Sun" which was recorded by Shaun Cassidy, "Little Miss American Dream" recorded by Toby Beau, "If You Can't Find Love" by the Oakridge Boys, and "Take Good Care of My Heart" by Jermaine Jackson and Whitney Houston.

- **Note from Rick Henry:** *"Last One Singin' the Blues" is such an excellent way to close such a fantastic album. It is easily one of my favorite songs on the album. The first time I listened to Karen's solo album I played it all the way through, and I enjoyed each and every track as if I had been there in 1979/80 while it was being recorded. Unlike my listening experience with a Carpenters album, I visualized Karen with a fearless grin on her face and an enthusiasm in her heart as she sang these songs. My impression after I listened to the album was one of awe. I fell in love with this record and have never grown tired of it since. My overall feeling is that Karen Carpenter really had a good time making this album, and you can hear it in her voice.*

Richard Carpenter - Pianist, Arranger, Composer, Conductor (click here to purchase)
Released: January 27, 1998
Producer: Richard Carpenter

Arrangements: Richard Carpenter
Background Vocals: Richard Carpenter, The OK Chorale, Karen Carpenter (Sandy)
Drums: Harvey Mason, Jim Gordon, Paul Liem, Karen Carpenter (Flat Baroque)
Keyboards and Piano: Richard Carpenter
Guitars: Tim May, Tony Peluso
Banjo: Tim May
Bass: Joe Osborn
Bassoon: Norm Herzberg
Tenor Sax: John Phillips (Time)
Oboe: Earle Dumler
English Horn: Earle Dumler
Clarinet: Jim Kanter
Flute: Sheridon Stokes
Recorder: Sheridon Stokes
Harmonica: Tommy Morgan
Synthesizer: Jeffery Vanston (C.J.)
Concertmaster: Jimmy Getzoff
Recorded at Capitol Studios
Engineers: Charlie Paakkari and Armin Steiner, except "Sandy" and "Flat Baroque," by Charlie Paakkari and Ray Gerhardt and "Time" by Roger Young
Assistants: Eric Cowden, Steve Genewick, Dan Thompson, Will Donavan
Mastered by: Bernie Grundman Mastering
Mixed at Capitol Studios by: Charlie Paakkari and Richard Carpenter
Art Direction/Design: Chuck Beeson
Photography: Reisig and Taylor
A very special thanks to: Ron Gorow without whose talents this album would have been much more difficult for all involved to have executed.
Dedicated to the memory of Agnes Carpenter, 1915-1996
Chart Positions: None
Certifications: None
Singles: Karen's Theme (1998), Medley (a shortened version)(1998)
Rick Henry's Rating: 5.5

"Pianist, Arranger, Composer, Conductor" is Richard Carpenter's second solo album. It's largely instrumental with a few backing vocals by Richard on the song "Time" and some vocals by Karen Carpenter on "Sandy." There are two new tunes, "Prelude" which opens the album and the touching "Karen's Theme," which closes the album. Overall, this album received lukewarm reviews from music reviewers and even from longtime Carpenters fans. Many people felt Richard Carpenter's re-recording of these classic Carpenters tunes was too easy-listening (even for Richard Carpenter). Some termed it as "elevator music." Many felt Richard should have recorded an album with new material instead. Despite the tepid response to this album, it is very well recorded with fine arrangements that live up to what one would expect from Richard Carpenter.

As the majority of this album is re-recordings of familiar songs I am only reviewing four songs, those being "Sandy," "Time," "Flat Baroque" and "Karen's Theme."

1. Sandy (Richard Carpenter/John Bettis) 3:50
    This is a very pleasant recording of the song yet leaves one wanting to hear Karen's lead vocal. The original, instrumental track was used for this song, minus Karen's lead vocal. In place of Karen's lead Richard added piano to guide the song, and the OK Chorale to add some extra, vocal harmonies. Karen's voice can be heard in this song as the original, backing vocals are used on this track. A nice mix of vocals toward the end makes this song a highlight. This song was originally recorded and released on the 1976 album "A Kind of Hush."

2. Time (Richard Carpenter) 3:55
    This is a nice remix of the original instrumental included on Richard Carpenter's 1987 album "Time."

3. Flat Baroque (Richard Carpenter) 1:51
    This new version of "Flat Baroque" is comprised mostly of the original instrumental track which was featured on the 1973 album "A Song for You." Karen Carpenter's original drum work, and Norm Herzberg's bassoon are surrounded with a new, livelier, piano track recorded

by Richard and added synthesizer parts by Jeffery
Vanston (CJ).

4.   Karen's Theme (Richard Carpenter) 2:40
       Many Carpenters fans consider this to be a Carpenters
       classic. Richard originally wrote the opening melody of
       this instrumental for use in the 1989 television movie
       "A Song for You: The Karen Carpenter Story." Richard
       completed the song in late 1996 for inclusion on this
       album. It was released as the lead single from the
       album although it did not chart.

As Time Goes By (click here to purchase)
Released: August 1, 2001 (Japan), April 13, 2004
(International)
Producer: Richard Carpenter
Arrangements, Orchestration & Conductor: Richard
Carpenter, Nelson Riddle (Without a Song, I Got Rhythm,
Karen/Ella Medley), Bobby Hammack (I Got Rhythm, You're
Just in Love), Paul Riser (Dancing in the Street), Roger Van
Epps (Dizzy Fingers), Peter Knight (Medley: Close
Encounters/Star Wars)
Vocals: Karen Carpenter, Richard Carpenter, OK Chorale
(Without a Song, You're Just in Love, The Rainbow
Connection), Ella Fitzgerald (Karen/Ella Medley), Perry Como
(Carpenters/Como Medley)
Drums: Karen Carpenter (I Got Rhythm, And When He Smiles),
Cubby O'Brien (Without a Song, I Got Rhythm, Dizzy Fingers,
You're Just in Love, Karen/Ella Medley, Carpenters/Como
Medley), Harvey Mason (Medley: Superstar/Rainy Days and
Mondays, California Dreamin', Hits Medley), Ron Tutt (Dancing
in the Street, Leave Yesterday Behind, The Rainbow
Connection)
Keyboards: Richard Carpenter, Pete Jolly (Karen/Ella Medley)
Guitar: Tony Peluso (You're Just in Love, Carpenters/Como
Medley, Hits Medley), Tim May (California Dreamin')
Steel Guitar: Jay Dee Maness (You're Just in Love)
Bass: Joe Osborn (Medley: Superstar/Rainy Days and
Mondays, Nowhere Man, Dancing in The Street, Leave
Yesterday Behind, Carpenters/Como Medley, California
Dreamin', The Rainbow Connection, Hits Medley), Chuck

Berfhofer (Without a Song, I Got Rhythm, Dizzy Fingers, You're Just in Love, Karen/Ella Medley), Bob Messenger (I Got Rhythm), Dan Woodhams (And When He Smiles)

Tenor Sax: Tom Scott (Dancing In The Street)

Baritone Sax: Jack Nimitz (California Dreamin')

Oboe: Earl Dumler (Medley: Superstar/Rainy Days and Mondays, Nowhere Man)

English Horn: Earle Dumler (Hits Medley)

Clarinet: Doug Strawn (Carpenters/Como Medley, And When He Smiles)

Flute: Sheridon Stokes (The Rainbow Connection, Hits Medley)

English Flute: Bob Messenger (And When He Smiles)

Recorder: Sheridon Stokes (The Rainbow Connection)

Flugelhorn: Buddy Childers (The Rainbow Connection, Hits Medley)

Banjo: Tim May (The Rainbow Connection)

Mandolin: Tim May (The Rainbow Connection)

Harmonica: Tom Morgan (Medley: Superstar/Rainy Days and Mondays, Nowhere Man, Leave Yesterday Behind)

Synthesizer: Tom Ranier (Carpenters/Como Medley, And When He Smiles)

Engineer: Roger Young (Without a Song, Medley: Superstar/Rainy Days and Mondays, I Got Rhythm, Dizzy Fingers, You're Just in Love, Karen/Ella Medley, The Rainbow Connection), John Hendrickson (Medley: Superstar/Rainy Days and Mondays, Nowhere Man, Dancing in the Street, You're Just in Love, Medley: Close Encounters/Star Wars, Leave Yesterday Behind, Carpenters/Como Medley, California Dreamin', Hits Medley), Ray Gerhardt (Dancing in The Street, Medley: Close Encounters/Star Wars, Leave Yesterday Behind, Carpenters/Como Medley, Hits Medley), Al Schmitt (Leave Yesterday Behind), Joe Osborn (California Dreamin'), Hugh Barker (And When He Smiles), Dave Iveland (Karen/Ella Medley, Dizzy Fingers, I Got Rhythm, Without a Song)

Mixed By: Richard Carpenter (All songs), Karen Carpenter (Without a Song, I Got Rhythm, Dizzy Fingers, Karen/Ella Medley), Dave Iveland (Without a Song, I Got Rhythm, Dizzy Fingers, Karen/Ella Medley), John Hendrickson (Medley: Superstar/Rainy Days and Mondays, Nowhere Man, Dancing in the Street, You're Just in Love, Medley: Close Encounters/Star Wars, Leave Yesterday Behind, Carpenters/Como Medley, California Dreamin', The Rainbow Connection, Hits Medley)

Recorded and Mixed at A&M Records and Capitol Studios, Hollywood, CA
Mastered by: Bernie Grundman
Design: Billy Mayfield
Photography: Annie Liebowitz (front cover)
Special Thanks: David Alley, Ron Gorow, John Hendrickson, Joe Osborn
Chart Positions: Japan #18
Certifications: Gold (Japan)
Singles: The Rainbow Connection
Rick Henry's Rating: 6.0

This release came as a surprise to most Carpenters fans as in 1989, with the release of "Lovelines." Richard Carpenter had announced there would be no further Carpenters releases.

The songs included on this album span the years 1967 to 1980. They come from various sources such as television specials, live performances, demos and outtakes. Richard Carpenter describes this collection as being one meant for the Carpentersphile.

The album was first released in Japan in 2001. Due to copyright discrepancies, the album's international release was delayed until 2004. By the time the album reached the US and European markets a large portion of die-hard Carpenters fans already owned a Japanese copy, so the album did not sell well and failed to chart in these countries. It did, however, make it to #18 in Japan, partly due to the demand from Europe and US fans.

1. Without A Song (Vincent Youmans / Billy Rose / Edward Eliscu) 1:58

> An edited one minute version of this track was first released in 1995 on the "Interpretations: 35th Anniversary Celebration" compilation. This song originally recorded in May 1980, for the Carpenters fifth television special "Music, Music, Music." At that point in time technology for music on television was still mixed in monaural sound. Karen and Richard were especially fond of the music used in this special that they decided to remix all the songs in stereophonic sound. After the

project was completed, of which Karen and Richard funded with their own money, they ended up with a few, reference discs which had never been heard by the general public until the release of "As Time Goes By." In the television version of this song Karen, Richard, Ella Fitzgerald and John Davidson did the vocal parts. When they remixed the song Karen sang Ella's parts and Richard did John's.

"Without a Song" was published in 1929 and used in the musical stage play "Great Day." Composer and Broadway producer, Vincent Youmans, is best known for the plays and films, "No, No, Nanette" (1925) and "Hit the Deck" (1927). His most popular songs include "Carioca," "Tea for Two," "Two Little Girls in Blue" and, of course, "Without a Song." Lyricist Billy Rose wrote the lyrics for the classics, "Me and My Shadow" (1927) and "It's Only a Paper Moon" (1933).

2. <u>Medley: Superstar/Rainy Days and Mondays (Bonnie Bramlett/ Leon Russell, Roger Nichols/Paul Williams)</u> 3:07
    This track was recorded in September 1976, for the Carpenters' Very First Television Special, which aired on December 8, 1976, and garnered huge ratings placing them at #6 in the Neilson ratings for that week.

    For its inclusion on "As Time Goes By" Richard Carpenter remixed parts of the medley so the entire piece of music would be in stereophonic sound. He also added an orchestra, Joe Osborn rerecorded his electric bass part and Tommy Morgan's ever-affecting harmonica was worked into the number.

3. <u>Nowhere Man (John Lennon / Paul McCartney)</u> 2:56
    Karen and Richard recorded this Beatles classic in 1967, in Joe Osborn's garage studio. Karen, at the young age of 17, sang this song with grace, ease and fantastic diction. She was already eons ahead of most singers at that age. Her voice already showed signs of depth and maturity, though she still had a ways to go before developing that famous Carpenter voice. Richard began reworking the

song in 1999, completing the arrangement the way he had envisioned years earlier. He put painstaking detail into getting every part perfect and blending the new arrangement into the already mixed mono recording. My viewpoint is that Richard Carpenter did an excellent job. The integration is seamless.

Before the release of "As Time Goes By" much speculation about the song circulated through Carpenters fan forums. Upon the album's release the song was an early favorite.

It was 1965 when John Lennon came up with "Nowhere Man." He worked on it for five hours before finally hitting on the right groove. He wanted to write something meaningful and deep. John Lennon was successful in writing such a beautiful song. Although the song is credited to John Lennon and Paul McCartney, it was John Lennon who wrote this timeless beauty. The song was released on the "Rubber Soul" album on the last day of December 1965. It was also featured in the 1968 film "Yellow Submarine." John Lennon, Paul McCartney and George Harrison sang the Beatles' recording in three-part harmony. The Beatles took the song to #4 in the UK and #3 in the US earning them a US Gold record.

4. <u>I Got Rhythm Medley (George and Ira Gershwin)</u> 4:43
    The "I Got Rhythm Medley" includes four, classic Gershwin tunes, those being "I Got Rhythm," "S'Wonderful," "Rhapsody in Blue" and "Fascinatin' Rhythm." This medley was recorded for the 1980 television special "Music, Music, Music" and was the opening production number of the show. It features a great drum solo from Karen Carpenter and a piano solo by Richard. Karen's vocal performance is spotless.

    Brothers George and Ira Gershwin are responsible for many more classics beyond the one in this medley, including: "Embraceable You," "They Can't Take That Away from Me," "Someone to Watch over Me," "Strike up the Band" and several others.

- **Note from Rick Henry:** *I really like this song quite a bit. It's one I usually come back to every few months or so. I've always been into rhythmic sort of tunes, and this one fits the bill. I really enjoy Karen's drum work.*
- **Additional side note:** *"S'Wonderful" and "Fascinatin' Rhythm" were both used in the fantastic drum solo Karen used to perform in concert during the mid-70's.*

5. <u>Dancing in the Street (Ivy Hunter / Marvin Gaye / William Stevenson)</u> 2:01
Karen and Richard had a love of Motown oldies. They put their stamp on three Motown songs including "Dancing in the Street," "Beechwood 4-5789" and the #1 hit "Please Mr. Postman." Sitting in the vaults of the unreleased is Karen's 1980 solo recording of "Jimmy Mack" bringing the total to four Motown songs of which Karen sang. "Dancing in the Street" is one of two Carpenters songs co-written by Marvin Gaye, the other is "Beechwood 4-5789."

The rendition of the song, which appears on "As Time Goes By", was recorded for the 1978 television special "Space Encounters" and was used as part of a medley. Richard Carpenter opted not to extend the arrangement and kept it as was recorded for the special, which explains the song's shortness in length. However, after some simple investigation, which was digging into the original Carpenters Fan Club Newsletter, it's discovered (or shall I say rediscovered) that Carpenters had, indeed, recorded a full-length studio version of the song. In a Q&A session in Newsletter #60 dated July 1978, a fan asked for info on the next, new album. Ev (Evelyn Wallace) kindly answered that it was hoped the album would be ready for release by the fall, and that some of the tracks would include "Little Girl Blue," "When I Fall in Love" and "Dancing in the Street." The first two songs have been released in their complete form though we're still waiting for the full version of "Dancing in the Street." In the same recording session a full-length, studio version of "Thank You for the Music" was recorded; this is another song which has yet to be released.

"Dancing in the Street" was originally recorded and released in 1964 by Martha and the Vandellas and has become a Motown signature tune. Martha and the Vandellas took the song to #2 in the US and #4 in the UK. Van Halen recorded their version in 1982 for their "Diver Down" album and reached the US Top 40 with their single release. Mick Jagger and David Bowie had a worldwide mega-hit with the song in 1985, reaching the Top 10 in about a dozen countries around the world including the US, UK, Australia, Ireland, Norway and others.

- **Note From Rick Henry:** *Short but sweet... this tune is fantastic; it's one of my favorites from the album. I just wish that one day the full-length, studio version recorded in 1978 would be released.*

6.   Dizzy Fingers (Edward Elzear "Zez" Confrey) 3:34
      Richard Carpenter had performed this ragtime tune in concert for several years as a solo. In 1980, the song was used in a segment of the television special "Music, Music, Music." In this segment Richard jumped from one piano to another. He dashed back and forth between six different pianos including two different grand pianos, harpsichord, toy piano, console piano and an upright piano. This segment gave Richard the opportunity to show off his talent as a pianist.

      Composer "Zez" Confrey wrote this ragtime instrumental "Dizzy Fingers" in 1923, and was one of Confrey's biggest hits. In 1921, Confrey wrote "Kitten on the Keys," which has ended up being his biggest hit. "Kitten on the Keys" was inspired by a cat at his grandmother's house that he discovered prancing up and down the piano keyboard. The song was later used in a Warner Bros. cartoon, "Rhapsody Rabbit," where Bugs Bunny and a mouse performed it as a duet.

- **Note from Rick Henry:** *This is one of the few Carpenters instrumentals that I really love. I can listen to this one over and over!*

7. <u>You're Just in Love (Irving Berlin)</u> 3:46
This is another outtake from the 1980 television special "Music, Music, Music." In total, five songs from that particular TV special ended up on "As Time Goes By." Originally the song was a duet between Karen Carpenter and John Davidson in the TV special, but for inclusion on this album Richard Carpenter replaced John's vocal with his own vocal. Many have felt the song should have been left with John Davidson's vocal. A year later, while recording the album "Made in America," Richard took the steel guitar intro to the song and applied it to "Those Good Old Dreams."

"You're Just in Love" written by the famed composer/lyricist Irving Berlin was first published in 1950 and was recorded by Perry Como with the Fontane Sisters. The song became a huge hit for them reaching #5 in the early part of 1951. A few weeks after the Como/Fontane release the song was also released by Rosemary Clooney & Guy Mitchell and Ethel merman & Dick Haymes; both duos made it into the US Top 30 with the song.

Irving Berlin has composed/written an endless amount of popular tunes including "Alexander's Ragtime Band," "Always," "Blue Skies," "Puttin' on the Ritz," "Cheek to Cheek," "Easter Parade," "I'm Puttin' All My Eggs in One Basket," "Let's Face the Music and Dance," "God Bless America," "Anything You Can Do," "There's No Business Like Show Business," "White Christmas" and many, many more.

- **Note from Rick Henry:** *I have always felt that this track may have been better had they left John Davidson's vocal intact. The syncing of Richard's vocal just does not seem to be 100% matched. It always seemed a little off to me.*

8.   <u>Karen / Ella Medley (various composers/writers)</u> 6:00
Featured in the 1980 television special "Music, Music, Music" this medley joins two of the world's finest interpreters of song. Ella Fitzgerald's vibrant energetic voice combined with Karen Carpenter's angelic deep and dark silky tones creates an irresistible pair of voices that are instantly recognizable and in their different styles are suited well to each other. The medley includes seven tunes (mostly songs that Ella recorded). It begins with "This Masquerade" (written by Leon Russell and was included on the Carpenters' 1973 album "Now & Then." The rest of the selections are songs Ella recorded: "My Funny Valentine" (Richard Rodgers, Lorenz Hart), "I'll Be Seeing You" (Sammy Fain, Irving Kahal), "Someone to Watch over Me" (George and Ira Gershwin), "As Time Goes By" (Herman Hupfeld), "Don't Get Around Much Anymore" (Duke Ellington, Bob Russell) and "I Let a Song Go out of My Heart" (Duke Ellington, Irving Mills).

Karen and Ella's vocals were recorded at different times and places. Karen recorded her vocals at A&M Recording Studios before the special, while Ella recorded her vocals live at the television studio. Richard Carpenter says Karen's pre-recorded vocal may have well been live as she got each song in one take. During the taping of the television special Richard and the engineers precisely synced Karen's voice to Ella's, and the result as we have all heard is pure magic.

- **Note from Rick Henry:** *This is easily my favorite track on the album. I especially like the way Karen sings "My Funny Valentine." Just to notate this, Sammy Fain and Irving Kahal, the writers of "I'll Be Seeing You," also wrote the classic tune "I Can Dream, Can't I?" which was featured on Carpenters' 1975 album "Horizon."*

9.   <u>Close Encounters/Star Wars Medley (John Williams)</u>
6:01

Arranged, conducted and orchestrated by the master Peter Knight for the 1980 television special "Music, Music, Music."

10. <u>Leave Yesterday Behind (Fred Karlin)</u> 3:34
The opening lines of this song are vaguely familiar to those of the 1971 meg-hit "For All We Know." There's a good reason for that as Fred Karlin who was a co-writer of "For All We Know" wrote the song.

Carpenters recorded "Leave Yesterday Behind" in 1978 for the television movie of the same name, which starred John Ritter, Carrie Fisher and Buddy Ebsen. The movie was about a young athlete, named Paul, whose life changed after an accident during a polo match, which left him paralyzed from the waist down. After the accident he moved to live on his father's ranch where he met Marnie, a horse trainer who fell for Paul. The movie aired on ABC TV on May 14, 1978. All five Carpenters television specials also appeared on the ABC TV network.

The song was recorded during the "Christmas Portrait" recording sessions and was intended to be released on what would have been a 10th Anniversary album in 1979. Instead, Richard checked himself into a clinic for his dependence on Quaaludes. He spent the better part of 1979 in Topeka, Kansas. Karen went on to record her solo album. Ironically, "Leave Yesterday Behind" was missed being released twice. First, when it was not used in the movie and second, when the 10th Anniversary album was left unfinished and shelved. Finally, the third time was the charm, and this 1978 tune was released in 2001 on the Japanese release of "As Time Goes By." In 2004 it received its worldwide release when "As Time Goes By" was released universally.

Karen's vocal performance on this track was a "work lead," recorded so that the bassist and drummer could sync their parts live instead of reading them from a music sheet. Once again Karen proves her vocal perfection with this first-take "work lead" which was not intended to appear on the final recording of this song.

Fred Karlin has composed more than 100 scores for theatrical films and television movies. His best known songs are "For All We Know" (Carpenters) and "Come Saturday Morning" (Sandpipers). Karlin won an Emmy Award for his score for the 1974 television film "The Autobiography of Miss Jane Pittman."

11.   Carpenters/Como Medley (Various songwriters) 6:56
This medley was featured in the 1974 Perry Como Christmas special in which Karen and Richard were guests. Other guests included Peggy Fleming and Rich Little. Due to the in-studio recording of Perry Como's parts, his vocals are rather distant and not of the best quality, which makes this medley uneven in sound quality. In the television special the medley was shortened down to five songs and ended with the song "Close to You." For this album Richard Carpenter decided to feature the full-length medley.

In this medley Carpenters sang Como songs and Como sang Carpenters songs alternating between each other. The medley ends with four Como songs. Many Carpenters fans have singled out Karen's performance of "It's Impossible" regarding it one of her best performances. Many fans wish Carpenters would have recorded the song in full length.

The songs in the medley include: "Yesterday Once More" (John Bettis, Richard Carpenter), "Magic Moments" (Burt Bacharach, Hal David), "Sing" (Joe Raposo), "Catch a Falling Star" (Lee Pockriss, Paul Vance), "Close to You" (Burt Bacharach, Hal David), "It's Impossible" (Armando Manzanero, Canche Manzanero, Sid Wayne), "We've Only Just Begun" (Paul Williams, Roger Nichols), "And I Love You So" (Don McLean), "Don't Let the Stars Get in Your Eyes" (Slim Willet), "'Till the End of Time" (Buddy Kaye, Ted Mossman), "No Other Love" (Richard Rodgers, Oscar Hammerstein II).

12.   California Dreamin' (John Phillips/Michelle Phillips)
2:33

This song was recorded in 1968, in Joe Osborn's garage studio. The original was recorded on four tracks with one track featuring Karen's vocal, and the other track had the music leaving two tracks open. In 1999, Richard took this song and transferred it from four tracks to 48 tracks and completely rerecorded the song from the bottom up. Richard claims this is one of his favorite tracks on "As Time Goes By" and describes Karen's vocal (at the age of 18) to be a marvel. He is especially taken by the way she jumps an octave, from chest voice, to head voice on the letter (and note) "A" in the opening.

"California Dreamin'" was a huge hit for The Mamas and The Papas having reached US #4 in 1966. John Phillips and his then wife, Michelle, wrote the tune in 1963. John Phillips claims the song came to him in a dream. He woke Michelle up, and she helped him write it. John and Michelle also wrote "Creeque Alley," "Monday, Monday" and a few other Mamas and Papas tunes.

13.   The Rainbow Connection (Paul Williams / Kenneth Ascher) 4:36

This popular "Muppet" song was recorded in 1980 during the "Made in America" recording sessions. Somehow, the existence of this song leaked to fans (even before the Internet was around), and for several years they had been writing to Richard requesting the release of the song. Again, this is a "work lead" perfectly performed by Karen. Along with "Leave Yesterday Behind," Richard completed work on this song in 1999, by adding extra vocals and orchestration.

"The Rainbow Connection" was released as a CD Single in Japan with "Leave Yesterday Behind" and "Hits Medley 76" as the B-side. The single reached #47 on the Japanese music charts.

"The Rainbow Connection" made its first appearance in 1979 when Kermit the Frog sang it in "The Muppet

Movie." The song received a 1979 Academy Award nomination for Best Original Song, but lost out to "It Goes Like It Goes" from the movie "Norma Rae." In 2004, the American Film Institute listed "The Rainbow Connection #74 on its list of the 100 best movie songs. Judy Garland's "Over the Rainbow" rightfully tops that list.

We all know the history behind one of its chief songwriters, Paul Williams, who has written/co-written such classics as "Rainy Days and Mondays," "Let Me Be the One," "I Won't Last a Day Without You," "We've Only Just Begun," "You and Me Against the World," "Evergreen (Love Theme from A Star is Born)," "An Old Fashioned Love Song" and several others. Kenneth Ascher is a jazz pianist who has scored many compositions and concertos dating back to 1960. He began working with Paul Williams in 1973 and wrote many songs with him until 1979, including collaborations on the soundtrack for the blockbuster film "A Star is Born."

14.   Hits Medley '76 (Various Songwriters) 8:13
The Hits Medley includes seven of Carpenters' most popular songs, including "Sing," "Close to You," "For All We Know," "Ticket to Ride," "Only Yesterday," "I Won't Last a Day Without You" and "Goodbye to Love." The medley was used for the closing segment of "Carpenters' Very First Television Special," which aired on ABC Television in December 1976.

15.   And When He Smiles (Hidden Track) (Al Anderson) 3:06

Released as a hidden track, "And When He Smiles" appeared at the end of the album with a gap of several seconds before it began playing. Karen and Richard recorded a track for it with Karen as drummer but never got around to recording a lead vocal for it. This studio track remains an instrumental. The recording featured on "As Time Goes By" was performed during the live, in-studio concert "Carpenters BBC Television Special 1971." Several of the songs for this TV Special were lip-synched, although "And When He Smiles" was recorded live during the program.

Richard heard the song as recorded by the Wildweeds, while on the road driving from one show to the next. The Wildweeds were a short-lived, garage band from Connecticut. They achieved one semi-hit called "No Good to Cry" in 1966. The song was mostly a regional hit on the East Coast, primarily Connecticut. "And When He Smiles" was released on the Wildweeds first and only album. Lead singer, guitarist and songwriter, Al Anderson left the band in 1971 and joined the more successful band NRBQ. Al Anderson wrote "And When He Smiles" as well as "No Good to Cry," "Mare Take Me Home" (recorded by Matthew's Southern Comfort Band), "Be My Woman Tonight" (B.W. Stevenson). Several country artists recorded Al's songs in the 90's including Carlene Carter, Dave Edmunds, Deborah Allen, Mavericks, Ty England, Deana Carter, Billy Ray Cyrus, Jerry Lee Lewis and many others.

Rick Henry's Favorite Carpenters/Karen Carpenter Songs (The List)
This list was going to be my Top 20 Favorites, but it ended up being my Top 22 Favorites... here goes...

22. Karen/Ella Medley
21. Rainy Days and Mondays
20. Home for the Holidays
19. Superstar
18. Make Believe It's Your First Time (Karen Solo)
17. Love Me for What I Am
16. Solitaire
15. Boat to Sail
14. One More Time
13. Please Mr. Postman
12. (I'm Caught Between) Goodbye and I Love You
11. A Song for You
10. Happy
 9. I Can't Make Music

8. If I Had You (Karen Solo)

7. Goodbye to Love

6. Road Ode

5. Desperado

4. Guess I Just Lost My Head (Karen Solo)

3. B'wana She No Home

2. This Masquerade

1. Only Yesterday

CPSIA information can be obtained
at www.ICGtesting.com
Printed in the USA
FSOW04n0958170816
23886FS